Dye It!
Paint It!
Quilt It!

OTHER BOOKS AVAILABLE FROM CHILTON

CONTEMPORARY QUILTING

All Quilt Blocks Are Not Square, by Debra Wagner
Barbara Johannah's Crystal Piecing
The Complete Book of Machine Quilting, Second Edition, by Robbie and Tony Fanning
Contemporary Quilting Techniques, by Pat Cairns
Creative Triangles for Quilters, by Janet B. Elwin
Fast Patch, by Anita Hallock
Precision Pieced Quilts Using the Foundation Method, by Jane Hall and Dixie Haywood
The Quilter's Guide to Rotary Cutting, by Donna Poster
Scrap Quilts Using Fast Patch, by Anita Hallock
Stars Galore and Even More, by Donna Poster
Stitch 'n' Quilt, by Kathleen Eaton
Super Simple Quilts, by Kathleen Eaton
Three-Dimensional Pieced Quilts, by Jodie Davis

CRAFT KALEIDOSCOPE

The Banner Book, Ruth Ann Lowery
The Crafter's Guide to Glues, Tammy Young
Creating and Crafting Dolls, by Eloise Piper and Mary Dilligan
Fabric Crafts and Other Fun with Kids, by Susan Parker Beck and Charlou Lunsford
Quick and Easy Ways with Ribbon, by Ceci Johnson
Learn Bearmaking, by Judi Maddigan
Stamping Made Easy, by Nancy Ward

CREATIVE MACHINE ARTS

ABCs of Serging, by Tammy Young and Lori Bottom
Affordable Heirlooms, by Edna Powers and Gaye Kriegel
Alphabet Stitchery by Hand & Machine, by Carolyn Vosburg Hall
The Button Lover's Book, by Marilyn Green
Claire Shaeffer's Fabric Sewing Guide
The Complete Book of Machine Embroidery, by Robbie and Tony Fanning
Craft an Elegant Wedding, by Tammy Young and Naomi Baker
Distinctive Serger Gifts and Crafts, by Naomi Baker and Tammy Young
Gail Brown's All-New Instant Interiors
Hold It! How to Sew Bags, Totes, Duffels, Pouches, and More, by Nancy Restuccia
How to Make Soft Jewelry, by Jackie Dodson
Innovative Serging, by Gail Brown and Tammy Young

The New Creative Serging Illustrated, by Pati Palmer, Gail Brown, and Sue Green
Quick Napkin Creations, by Gail Brown
Second Stitches: Recycle as You Sew, by Susan Parker
Serge a Simple Project, by Tammy Young and Naomi Baker
Serge Something Super for Your Kids, by Cindy Cummins
Sew Any Patch Pocket, by Claire Shaeffer
Sew Any Set-In Pocket, by Claire Shaeffer
Sew Sensational Gifts, by Naomi Baker and Tammy Young
Sewing and Collecting Vintage Fashions, by Eileen MacIntosh
Shirley Botsford's Daddy's Ties
Soft Gardens: Make Flowers with Your Sewing Machine, by Yvonne Perez-Collins
The Stretch & Sew Guide to Sewing Knits, by Ann Person
Twenty Easy Machine-Made Rugs, by Jackie Dodson
The Ultimate Serger Answer Guide, by Naomi Baker, Gail Brown, and Cindy Kacynski

SEW AND SERGE SERIES,
BY JACKIE DODSON

Sew & Serge Pillows! Pillows! Pillows!
Sew & Serge Terrific Textures

KNOW YOUR SERGER SERIES,
BY TAMMY YOUNG AND NAOMI BAKER

Know Your baby lock

STARWEAR

Dazzle, by Linda Fry Kenzle
Embellishments, by Linda Fry Kenzle
Jan Saunders' Wardrobe Quick-Fixes
Make It Your Own, by Lori Bottom and Ronda Chaney
Mary Mulari's Garments with Style
A New Serge in Wearable Art by Ann Boyce
Pattern-Free Fashions, by Mary Lee Trees Cole
Shirley Adams' Belt Bazaar
Sweatshirts with Style, by Mary Mulari

TEACH YOURSELF TO SEW BETTER,
BY JAN SAUNDERS

A Step-by-Step Guide to Your New Home
A Step-by-Step Guide to Your Sewing Machine

DYE IT!
PAINT IT!
QUILT IT!

MAKING AND USING ONE-OF-A-KIND FABRICS IN QUILTS

Joyce Mori

Cynthia Myerberg

Chilton
BOOK COMPANY
RADNOR, PENNSYLVANIA

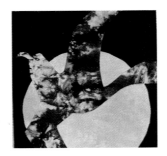

PUBLISHED IN RADNOR, PENNSYLVANIA 19089,
BY CHILTON BOOK COMPANY

**Quilt blocks on the front cover
(left to right, from top):**
Hunter's Star Block by Pat Hill,
May Basket by Dianna Parsons,
Beach Party by Pam Kelson,
Rocky Mountain by Marty Ayersman,
Brotherly Love by Dee Bronson,
Ohio Star by Barb Pavlovic,
an original design by Joyce Mori, and
Churn Dash by Kitty Morgan.

Designed by Stan Green/Green Graphics

Illustrations by Maricris Joy Roque,
Betsy Noullet, and Susan Marsh

Photographs by Edward A. Petrosky, West
Virginia University Publications Services

Manufactured in the United States of America

Library of Congress
Cataloging-in-Publication Data

Mori, Joyce.
    Dye it! paint it! quilt it! : making and using
one-of-a-kind fabrics in quilts / Joyce Mori,
Cynthia Myerberg.
        p.   cm.
    Includes index.
    ISBN 0-8019-8737-7 (pb)
    1. Quilting. 2. Dyes and dyeing—Textile
fibers. 3. Textile painting. I. Myerberg,
Cynthia. II. Title.
TT835.M682   1996   95-53849
746.6—dc20   CIP
        1 2 3 4 5 6 7 8 9 0   5 4 3 2 1 0 9 8 7 6

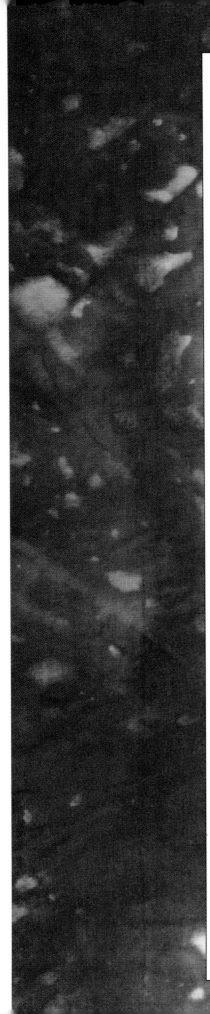

CONTENTS

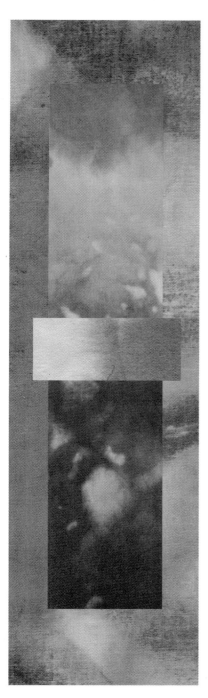

ACKNOWLEDGMENTS

Joyce Mori and Cynthia Myerberg wish to thank:

• The Chilton Book Company for their support of this book. Chilton books support and develop the creativity of quilters by making available new skills and techniques that help make quilting projects beautiful and exciting. Special thanks to Robbie Fanning for getting us started on this book idea. Susan Keller, the developmental editor, has aided greatly in the organization, editing, and problem-solving involved in creating the book.

• All of the quilters who participated in the challenge block section of the book, for their original ideas that never failed to amaze us. Most of these quilters had never used dyed or painted fabrics before, but they jumped in and willingly tried something new. We offer to them a tremendous THANK YOU. All the readers of this book will benefit from their efforts.

• The photographer, Ed Petrosky, and graphic artists, Joy Roque, Betsy Noullet, and Susan Marsh, for making this book colorful and the directions easy to follow.

Joyce Mori offers the following thanks

I had been dyeing and painting fabric for several years before taking a week-long workshop from Jan Myers-Newbury. Seeing her love of dyed fabrics, her creation of wonderful colors, and her gradation method of dyeing pushed me to make and use these fabrics in many of my quilts. My intense "immersion" into the dyeing process led to the conception of this book. (For more information about Jan Myers-Newbury's workshop schedule, send a self-addressed stamped envelope to her at 7422 Ben Hur Street, Pittsburgh, PA 15208.)

My husband John gets my love and thanks for putting up with all my manuscript deadlines and extra work necessary to write a book.

I thank God for the opportunity to work at something I love.

Last, but not least, I owe fate thanks for putting Cynthia in my dyeing workshop and having us discover we were both interested in quilting, creativity, and writing. Our backgrounds are different and our quilts very different, but our mutual interests and friendship made the book possible.

Cynthia Myerberg offers the following thanks

To my mother, Marie Ewers Torrence, for teaching me to sew and encouraging me to be creative.

To my father, the late James J. Torrence, a role model from whom I learned a strong work ethic and the importance of "measure twice, cut once."

To my husband, David, and our family, Nalini and Ramani Pillai and Jonah and Zachary Myerberg, for being supportive and helpful in so many ways.

To Jan Myers-Newbury for giving me the tool that has added a new dimension to my quilt making.

To Joyce Mori, my friend and mentor, for her patience, wisdom, and guidance in helping me write my first book.

PREFACE

Creating quilts using traditional quilt patterns can give you a sense of connection with the quilters of the past and a feeling of being part of the long tradition of quilting. However, you may sometimes get the urge to give your quilts a modern twist and to add your creative input to the ever-evolving quilting tradition. One way to act on this creative impulse is to use unique hand-dyed or hand-painted fabrics to give traditional quilt patterns a fresh look and bring them into the 21st century.

You may think that creating your own fabric is difficult and requires special artistic skills, but as you try some of the projects in this book you will see that that's not the case. We provide complete, easy-to-follow directions for immersion dyeing, direct dyeing, and tie dyeing that will enable you to create truly beautiful original fabrics. The techniques are fun and satisfying, and they provide a wonderful form of creative expression. In addition, you can produce a range of colors and values far greater than what is available commercially.

We also show you how you can use inexpensive, readily available paints to design lovely one-of-a-kind fabrics. Fabric painting is fun, and many of the techniques are so easy they can be done by children.

The fabrics you make with dyes and paints can be used alone, or they can be combined with purchased fabrics of your choice. Some quilters may at first be intimidated by the prospect of incorporating hand-dyed and hand-painted fabrics into their quilts, but there really is no mystery to it. To help you become comfortable with these fabrics quickly, we introduce them into traditional quilt blocks and show you many examples of hand-dyed and hand-painted fabrics giving such blocks a bright, contemporary look.

HOW TO USE THIS BOOK

The focus of this book is incorporating the special look of dyed and painted fabrics to update traditional quilts and to energize other fabric projects. To this end, we provide plenty of useful information for those who may choose to skip the dyeing and painting processes altogether, opting instead to buy fabrics with a similar look that are available commercially or from individual craftspeople. We should also note that although this book is for quilters, it does not cover the basics of quiltmaking; that is, the quilting instructions tend to emphasize how specific

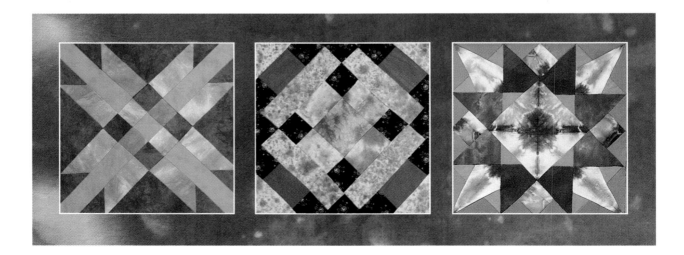

blocks are put together rather than describing general quilt construction.

After covering the basics of dyeing and painting fabrics, we treat you to a special chapter filled with "challenge blocks" contributed by quilters of all skill levels. We gave these quilters, many of whom had never used dyed and painted fabric before, packets of such fabric to use (along with commercial fabrics, if they wished) to design their own quilt blocks. The resulting blocks, which illustrate a wide range of color schemes, block patterns, and fabric choices, show how much fun it can be to combine dyed and painted fabrics with a little imagination. We hope they inspire you as you design your own blocks.

The chapter following the challenge blocks provides various wall quilt projects with step-by-step instructions for cutting and piecing. The projects range in skill level from beginner to advanced, and they feature fabrics made using many of the techniques explored in this book. You may choose to try to duplicate these quilts

right down to the fabric colors and patterns, or you may choose to use them as a stepping-off place from which to let your own preferences and instincts guide you. If you wish, use the line drawings provided in Appendix D to help you create original designs. Just photocopy the drawing several times and then color each one with various patterns and colors until you get a combination that pleases you.

The last chapter in this book features lovely wearable art and gift ideas. Your favorite clothing patterns and craft projects can be made using your own dyed or painted fabric. Even the simplest vest takes on a designer look when made or accented with your original fabric creations!

This book provides you with the techniques for dyeing and painting fabric and shows you how to use this fabric in traditional quilt blocks as well as in other items. Although the dyeing and painting techniques we describe are for beginners, the results are purely professional and can take you beyond tradition to a new dimension in quilting.

These are some of the lovely fabrics you can learn to create following the directions presented in this chapter.

IMMERSION DYEING AND DIRECT DYEING

This chapter presents the direct dyeing and immersion dyeing techniques used to create the fabrics shown in this book. The step-by-step directions given in this chapter are the basic directions for all of the dyeing techniques and dyeing variations mentioned in this book.

Read all of these directions carefully before you begin any dyeing adventure.

Overview of Dyeing Techniques

IMMERSION DYEING

Immersion dyeing generally produces fabric that is solid in color. You can also use this method to produce fabrics with value gradations, mottled effects, and tie-dye patterns.

For the immersion technique, damp fabric is immersed in a dye bath of water, dye, and salt. The salt encourages the fibers of the fabric to absorb the dye. The dye bath must be stirred fre-quently to insure that the dye solution reaches all surfaces of the fabric.

Dye activator or soda ash is added to the dye bath to create a permanent bond between the dye molecules and the fiber. After the dye activator is added, the fabric remains in the dye bath for 1 hour to achieve maximum color absorption. (Frequent stirring and rearranging of the fabric insures smooth, evenly colored fabric; mottled and tie-dyed fabrics are stirred less fre-

2

quently.) The fabric is then rinsed in warm water and washed in hot water and Synthrapol SP (described below) to remove any remaining unfixed dye molecules.

DIRECT DYEING

You can use the direct dyeing method to produce an array of patterned, textured, and multi-colored fabrics. The fabric is presoaked in a solution of water, salt, and dye activator. Presoaked fabric may then be dyed wet, damp, or dry. The dye solution is randomly poured, sprayed, or dripped onto the fabric. The fabric is then covered with plastic and left to cure for 3 to 24 hours. After curing, the fabric is rinsed and washed as described above in the directions for immersion dyeing.

Basic Preparations

DYEING SUPPLIES AND SOURCES

Mail-order sources for these dyes, chemicals, and fabrics are listed in Appendix A.

DYE

Procion MX fiber-reactive dye, the dye we used to do the projects in this book, is synthetic, nontoxic, and fiber-reactive. The dye molecules react with the molecules of the fiber to produce a permanent, colorfast, and lightfast bond. These dyes produce bright, even colors from pastel to vibrant hues. Procion dye colors mix well with one another to produce many new colors. *Procion dye will dye only natural fibers.* If you attempt to dye a blend of natural and synthetic fibers such as cotton/polyester, only the cotton fibers will take the dye. The resulting fabric will have a lighter value than it would have if it were all-cotton, or it will have a heathered look.

Procion dyes react best in water temperatures of 70°F to 105°F. Water that is too hot may destroy the reactivity of the dye. Water that is too cold may slow down or even stop the reaction of the dye with the fiber. If you leave direct-dyed fabric to cure in a room that is below 65°F, the reaction may stop altogether.

Procion dyes are nontoxic and will not harm the environment. Dye solutions may be disposed of by pouring them down the drain if you are on a sewer line or have a septic system that is below ground. Contact your local water service for disposal advice if you have a wastewater system other than the above-mentioned types.

Procion dyes may be purchased in 2-ounce, 8-ounce, 1-pound, 5-pound, and even up to 110-pound containers. Most dye supply houses offer a sampler kit containing six to eight 2-ounce containers of dye; however, for the serious dyer, the 8-ounce or 1-pound jars are more economical.

Powdered dyes may be stored in a closed container in a cool, dry place for several years. Once mixed with water, they can be stored in the refrigerator for about 2 weeks. Once dye activator has been added to the dye solution, the life of the solution is less than 1 hour. This is why a dye bath that has been used for immersion dyeing cannot be reused.

WATER SOFTENER

Hard water can interfere with the dyeing process and cause dull, uneven, or mottled colors. If you have hard water, you can avoid these problems by using water softener. Use 1 teaspoon of water softener for every quart of water in the dye bath. Calgon water softener is available at supermarkets; other softeners are available through dye supply sources.

SYNTHRAPOL SP

Synthrapol SP is an economical, nonalkaline, industrial-strength detergent that is highly recommended for use with dyed fabric. Synthrapol SP is used as a prewash and an afterwash. When used as an afterwash, it keeps loose dye particles in suspension so that they do not stain other areas of the fabric.

FABRIC

Only 100% natural-fiber fabrics (cotton, silk, viscous rayon, and linen) that do not have permanent-press, press-care, crease-resistant, or stain-resistant finishes can be effectively dyed with Procion MX dyes using the methods described in this book. Permanent-press fabric does not absorb the dye as well as non-permanent-press fabric does, and dyeing such fabric produces a lighter value of the desired color. Mercerized, non-permanent-press fabric is excellent for dyeing because it has outstanding color absorption, but it is not necessary to buy such fabric, because nonmercerized fabric works well, too. The methods we describe in this book work best for 100% cotton and 100% viscous rayon. You can dye 100% silk by the same methods, but the resulting colors will not be as bright as the colors produced by the same dyes used on cotton or rayon. All of the quilt projects shown use 100% cotton fabric. Viscous rayon and silk are used for some of the clothing and gifts.

All fabric must be prescoured to remove starch, sizing, and oils. (Note that prescouring will not remove a permanent-press finish.) To prescour the fabric, machine-wash it on the hottest setting with 1 teaspoon Synthrapol SP and 1 teaspoon dye activator per 3 yards of fabric. Use proportional amounts of Synthrapol SP and dye activator for larger quantities of fabric. Machine-dry the fabric and store it until you are ready to use it. Or, if you are ready to use it right away, place it in the dye bath while it is still damp.

DYE ACTIVATOR

Procion MX dye requires an alkali to fix the color. Dye activator is an alkali that increases the pH of the dye bath and causes the dye molecules to bond permanently with the molecules of the fiber. (You can also use soda ash—sodium carbonate—for this purpose.) For immersion dyeing, dye activator is dissolved in hot water and then added to the dye bath. For the direct method of dyeing, dye activator is a component of the presoak solution. Dye activator can be purchased through dye supply houses. Soda ash can be purchased at pool supply distributors. Do not use washing soda purchased at the supermarket, as it may contain whiteners or bleach.

SALT

Noniodized salt is added to the dye bath to encourage the fibers to absorb more dye. (Do not use iodized salt, which can cause dull colors.) The salt is dissolved in the water of the dye bath before the dye is added. Noniodized salt or canning salt can be purchased in large quantities from supermarkets and farm supply stores.

DYEING UTENSILS

All utensils used for dyeing should be kept separate from kitchen utensils and should never be used for food preparation. Yard sales and flea markets are great places to purchase utensils for dyeing.

PLASTIC BUCKETS

You will need one bucket for each color or value of a color that you plan to dye. Also, it is helpful to have several extra buckets for soaking and rinsing. The white 5-gallon buckets available from restaurants and wallpaper hangers are the best, and they are usually free. A 2-gallon bucket is the smallest useful size. Do not use metal buckets.

PLASTIC OR GLASS MEASURING CONTAINERS

You will need at least one large (1- or 2-gallon) measuring container. You will also need several graduated measuring containers with pouring spouts: two 1-cup, two 2-cup, and one 4-cup.

PLASTIC MEASURING SPOONS

You will need two or three sets of plastic measuring spoons that measure from 1/8 teaspoon to 1 tablespoon.

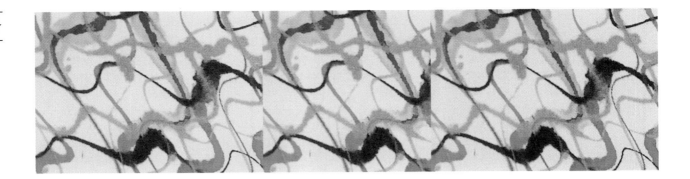

PLASTIC SPOONS

You will need a variety of sizes of plastic spoons for stirring and mixing dye and dye activator.

PLASTIC OR GLASS CONTAINERS

You will need two dozen 8- to 16-ounce yogurt containers, jelly glasses, and/or plastic drinking cups for mixing the dye or dye activator solutions. A few jars with lids are needed to store any leftover dye solution.

PLASTIC DROP CLOTH

Plastic dry-cleaner bags or garbage bags or a plastic drop cloth can be used to cover a surface used for direct dyeing.

PLASTIC BAGS

You can use plastic grocery bags or shopping bags to hold direct-dyed fabric while it is curing.

DIRECT-DYE APPLICATORS

Plastic spoons, eyedroppers, spray bottles, squirt bottles, sponges, utility brushes, syringes, and so on can be used for direct dyeing.

RUBBER GLOVES

Heavy latex kitchen gloves are the best. Do not use short disposable medical gloves.

OLD CLOTHES, OLD SHOES, AND AN APRON

Dress appropriately, and don't forget to change your shoes!

DUST MASK

Always wear a NIOSH-approved dust mask designed for protection against organic dust.

They cost about $1.60 each and are reusable. They are available at most hardware stores and paint supply stores, as well as from the dye supply sources listed in Appendix A.

KITCHEN TIMER

Use a kitchen timer to remind yourself to stir the dye bath.

SAFETY CONSIDERATIONS

• Take care not to inhale or ingest dye powder or dye activator. Wear a dust mask when mixing dry chemicals, and avoid getting the chemicals into your eyes. Minimize airborne particles by opening only one jar of dye at a time; also, avoid excess stirring or manipulating of the dry powder.

• Both the powder form and the solution form of dye can stain the skin. Always wear old clothes, old shoes, and rubber gloves when working with dye. Dye activator in powder or solution may cause skin irritation, so wear rubber gloves when working with this substance.

• **If you are pregnant, do not handle the dry chemicals.** Have someone else mix the dye powder and dye activator into solution for you.

• Always label stored dye solutions, and keep all dyes and chemicals, either dry or in solution, out of the reach of children and pets. Do not smoke, eat, or drink in the area where you are dyeing.

Directions for Immersion Dyeing

These directions for immersion dyeing are for ½-yard lengths of fabric. If you wish to dye 1-yard lengths, double all measurements for dye, water, and activator. *The only factor that will not double is the time that the fabrics are in the dye bath.* Please read the overview of the dyeing process and all directions before starting.

Dyeing Process

1. PRESCOUR FABRIC: Machine-wash the fabric on the hot cycle with 1 teaspoon Synthrapol SP and 1 teaspoon dye activator per 3 yards of fabric. Keep the fabric damp if dyeing immediately; however, fabric may be prescoured, machine-dried, and stored for future dyeing. Prior to dyeing, thoroughly wet the fabric with water and wring it out. (In immersion dyeing, fabric is dampened before it is added to the dye bath to ensure even coloring of the fabric.)

2. MIX DYE SOLUTIONS: *Put on rubber gloves and a dust mask.* Dissolve the dye powder in ¼ cup of warm water (70°F to 105°F) in a graduated 1-cup container. Stir until all the powder is dissolved and a paste is formed. Add more water if the paste is too thick. Then add water to this dye paste to make 1 cup of dye solution.

APPROXIMATE AMOUNTS OF DYE POWDER NEEDED FOR A 1-GALLON DYE BATH AND ½ YARD OF FABRIC

Shade	Dye Powder
light shade	1 teaspoon
medium shade	3 teaspoons
dark shade	6 teaspoons

3. PREPARE DYE ACTIVATOR SOLUTION: In a small plastic container, completely dissolve 2 tablespoons of dye activator in 1 cup of hot water. Prepare 1 cup of dye activator solution for each dye bucket. Set a cup of the dissolved dye activator solution next to each dye bucket.

You may now remove your dust mask, but continue to wear your gloves until you have finished the dyeing process.

SUPPLIES NEEDED

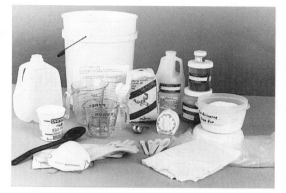

1-1 Supplies required for immersion dyeing.

½-yard lengths of 100% natural-fiber fabrics (one ½-yard length of fabric for each color to be dyed)

Procion MX fiber-reactive dye

Synthrapol SP

Noniodized salt

Dye activator or soda ash

Old clothes, old shoes, and an apron

Dust mask

Rubber gloves

Plastic buckets (2- to 5-gallon size), one bucket for each color or value to be dyed

Glass or plastic 1- and 2-cup graduated measuring containers with pouring spouts

1-gallon measuring container (glass or plastic) such as a plastic milk jug

Plastic measuring spoons

Plastic stirring spoons

Small plastic containers (8- to 16-ounce size) such as yogurt containers or drinking cups

Kitchen timer

4. FILL BUCKETS: Pour 1 gallon of warm water (70°F to 105°F) into each dye bucket.

5. ADD SALT: Add ½ cup of salt to each dye bucket and stir until dissolved.

6. ADD DYE: Add the dye solution to each dye bucket and stir with gloved hand.

7. ADD FABRIC: Add a ½-yard length of damp fabric to each dye bucket. Do not add more than ½-yard of fabric to a 1-gallon dye bath. Stir with gloved hand for 5 minutes and push out the air bubbles. Try to keep the fabric submerged. When all the fabric has been added to each dye bucket and stirred, set the timer for 10 minutes. Thoroughly stir each dye bucket (for approximately 1 minute) every 10 minutes during the next 30 minutes. Use a kitchen timer and follow the chart on page 7 as you complete the remainder of the steps.

8. ADD DYE ACTIVATOR: After 30 minutes, add the dissolved dye activator solution to each dye bucket. Be careful not to pour the solution directly onto the fabric. Stir each dye bucket for 1 minute, rearranging the fabric frequently. When the dye activator solution has been added to all of the dye buckets and all have been stirred, set the timer for 10 minutes. Thoroughly stir each dye bucket every 10 minutes for the next 60 minutes.

9. RINSE: Remove the fabric from the dye buckets at the end of 60 minutes. Thoroughly rinse the fabric in warm water to remove the excess dye solution.

10. AFTERWASH: Machine-wash the fabrics in hot water with 2 tablespoons of Synthrapol SP, which allows just-dyed fabrics to be washed together without exchanging dye. The dye will not remain in your machine or stain subsequent laundry. Machine-dry the fabric. Dry fabric will appear several shades lighter than wet fabric.

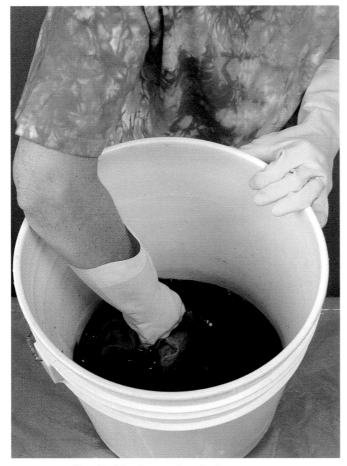

Step 7 of the immersion dyeing process, in which the fabric is stirred in a dye bucket.

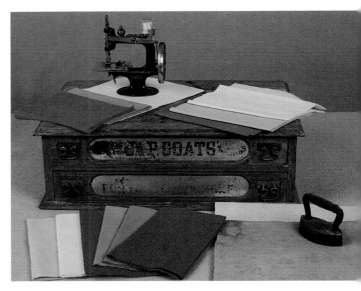

These are some of the lovely fabrics created with the immersion dyeing method and an immersion dyeing variation that produces mottled fabric.

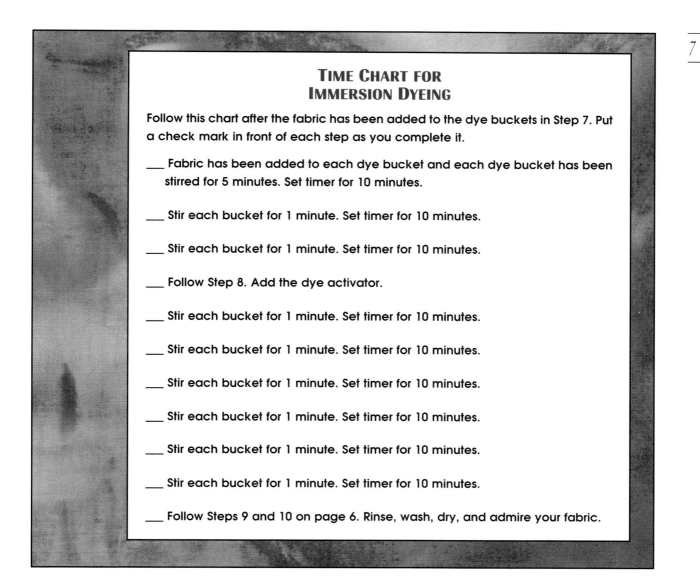

TIME CHART FOR IMMERSION DYEING

Follow this chart after the fabric has been added to the dye buckets in Step 7. Put a check mark in front of each step as you complete it.

___ Fabric has been added to each dye bucket and each dye bucket has been stirred for 5 minutes. Set timer for 10 minutes.

___ Stir each bucket for 1 minute. Set timer for 10 minutes.

___ Stir each bucket for 1 minute. Set timer for 10 minutes.

___ Follow Step 8. Add the dye activator.

___ Stir each bucket for 1 minute. Set timer for 10 minutes.

___ Stir each bucket for 1 minute. Set timer for 10 minutes.

___ Stir each bucket for 1 minute. Set timer for 10 minutes.

___ Stir each bucket for 1 minute. Set timer for 10 minutes.

___ Stir each bucket for 1 minute. Set timer for 10 minutes.

___ Stir each bucket for 1 minute. Set timer for 10 minutes.

___ Follow Steps 9 and 10 on page 6. Rinse, wash, dry, and admire your fabric.

IMMERSION DYEING: MOTTLED AND TIE-DYE VARIATION

Mottled and tie-dyed fabrics can add interest and flair to a quilting project and make it truly one of a kind. Mottled and tie-dyed fabrics are created using the immersion dyeing method with a few changes, as noted in the directions below. One other change: Since it is not necessary for the dye solution to reach all areas of mottled or tie-dyed fabric, up to 2 yards of fabric can be dyed in a 1-gallon dye bath. (For more on tie dyeing, see Chapter 2, "Tie Dyeing and Shibori-Wrap Dyeing.")

Dyeing Process

STEPS 1 THROUGH 6. Follow Steps 1 through 6 on pages 5–6.

NEW STEP 7. After you have placed the fabric in the dye bath, stir the dye bucket only one time during the first 30 minutes.

NEW STEP 8. After adding the dye activator, stir the dye bucket only two times during the next 60 minutes.

STEPS 9 AND 10. Finish the process by following Steps 9 and 10 on page 6.

Nine-Step Immersion-Dyed Gradated Sequence

Achieving a full range of values of a color (from darkest to lightest) can best be accomplished by dyeing nine gradations of that color. You will then be able to see a gradual range from the darkest value of that color to the lightest value. If you later choose to dye fewer than nine gradations, you can then decide which value levels from values one to nine you'd like to skip.

SUPPLIES NEEDED

4½ yards of 100% natural-fiber fabric cut into ½-yard lengths

Procion MX fiber-reactive dye

Synthrapol SP

Noniodized salt

Dye activator or soda ash

Old clothes, old shoes, and an apron

Rubber gloves

Dust mask

Nine 2- to 5-gallon plastic buckets

Several glass or plastic 1- and 2-cup graduated measuring containers with pouring spouts

One 1-gallon measuring container (glass or plastic) such as a plastic milk jug

Plastic measuring spoons

Plastic spoons for stirring and mixing

Nine 8- to 16-ounce plastic containers such as yogurt containers or drinking cups

Kitchen timer

The following instructions are for dyeing nine gradations of one color using ½-yard lengths of fabric. Each value level is dyed in its own dye bucket.

Gradation dyeing goes much faster if you have a friend, preferably a quilter, to help you. Be sure to use a time chart: it is easy to forget how many times the nine buckets have been stirred if you are having too much fun!

This is the method of gradation dyeing taught by Jan Myers-Newbury in her workshops (see the Acknowledgments for more information).

Dyeing Process

Before you begin, please read pages 1–4 ("Overview of Dyeing Techniques" through "Safety Considerations") and all of the steps that follow.

1. PRESCOUR FABRIC: Machine-wash the fabric on the hot cycle with 1½ teaspoons Synthrapol SP and 1½ teaspoons dye activator. Keep the fabric damp if dyeing immediately. Fabric may be prescoured, machine-dried, and stored for future dyeing. If you choose to store the fabric, wet it thoroughly with water and wring it out prior to dyeing.

2. MIX DYE SOLUTION: Put on rubber gloves and a dust mask.

In a 2-cup or 4-cup measuring container, dissolve the dye powder in ¼ cup of warm water (70°F to 105°F). Stir until all the powder is dissolved. Add more water if this paste is too thick. Then add enough water to this dye paste to make 2 cups of dye solution.

APPROXIMATE AMOUNTS OF DYE POWDER NEEDED FOR NINE VALUES OF VARIOUS COLORS*

Color	Amount
Red	1 tablespoon
Green	3 tablespoons
Blue	3 tablespoons
Black or Navy	6 tablespoons
Yellow	6 tablespoons

*See Appendix C for more dye recipes.

3. PREPARE DYE ACTIVATOR SOLUTION: In a plastic drinking cup or yogurt container, thoroughly dissolve 2 tablespoons of dye activator in 1 cup of hot water. Prepare nine of these cups. Set a cup of the dissolved dye activator solution next to each dye bucket. You may now remove your dust mask, but continue to wear your gloves until you have finished the dyeing process.

4. FILL BUCKETS: Pour 1 gallon of warm water (70° to 105°F) into each dye bucket. All buckets should contain water that is approximately the same temperature to ensure smooth, even gradations.

5. ADD SALT: Add ½ cup of salt to each dye bucket and stir until dissolved.

6. ADD THE DYE SOLUTION TO EACH BUCKET IN THE FOLLOWING MANNER: Have a 2-quart container of warm water available. You are starting with 2 cups of dye solution. Measure out 1 cup of this dye solution and pour it into the first dye bucket. This is your darkest value.

You now have 1 cup of dye solution left. Add 1 cup of clear room-temperature water to this remaining dye solution. Now you have 2 cups of dye solution that is half as strong as the dye solution that went into the first dye bucket. Stir this dye solution, then put 1 cup of this new dye solution into the second bucket. Now add 1 cup of room-temperature water to your remaining dye solution. Continue this process, putting 1 cup of dye solution into the next bucket and replacing it with 1 cup of water until you have added dye to all nine buckets (or to your last bucket). You will be left with 1 cup of very light dye solution. You

may discard it or use it to create a still lighter fabric. (Or save it to create neutral fabrics; see page 14.) Stir each bucket.

7. ADD FABRIC: Add a ½-yard length of the prescoured, dampened fabric to each dye bucket. Do not add more than ½ yard of fabric to a 1-gallon dye bath. Stir each dye bucket with your gloved hand for 5 minutes and push out any air bubbles. Try to keep the fabric submerged. When all the fabric has been added and stirred, set the timer for 10 minutes. Thoroughly stir each dye bucket (for approximately 1 minute) every 10 minutes during the next 30 minutes. Use a kitchen timer and follow the chart on page 7.

8. ADD DYE ACTIVATOR: Thirty minutes after you place the fabrics in the dye baths, add the dissolved dye activator solution to each dye bucket. Be careful not to pour the solution directly onto the fabric. Stir each dye bucket for 1 minute, rearranging the fabric frequently. After the dye activator solution has been added to each of the dye buckets and all the buckets have been stirred, set the timer for 10 minutes. Thoroughly stir each dye bucket every 10 minutes for the next 60 minutes. Remember to check off the steps on the chart, as mentioned in Step 7.

9. RINSE: Remove the fabric from the dye buckets at the end of the 60 minutes specified in Step 8. Thoroughly rinse the fabric in warm water to remove the excess dye solution.

10. AFTERWASH: Machine-wash the fabrics in hot water with 2 tablespoons of Synthrapol SP and then machine-dry.

IMMERSION GRADATION DYEING: SKIPPED VALUE VARIATION

If you prefer to dye fewer than nine values of a color, you may skip any of the values between one and nine. Decide which values you wish to skip, then follow the directions on the next page.

These fabrics were dyed using the nine-step immersion dyeing method and the skipped-value immersion dyeing method.

Dyeing Process

1. Set out a bucket for each value to be dyed.

2. Where a value is to be skipped, place a small container that holds at least 8 ounces in place of the bucket. (Thus, you will have a total of nine containers set out, including the buckets and smaller containers.)

3. Follow Steps 1 and 2 for the "Nine-Step Immersion-Dyed Gradated Sequence" on pages 8–9.

4. Prepare 1 cup of dye activator solution according to the directions on page 5 for each value to be dyed, and place one cup next to

each bucket. You may now remove your dust mask, but continue to wear your gloves until you have finished the dyeing process.

5. Follow Steps 4 and 5 for the "Nine-Step Immersion-Dyed Gradated Sequence" on page 9.

6. Follow Step 6 for the "Nine-Step Immersion-Dyed Gradated Sequence" on page 9, adding the dye to the dye buckets as directed. When you get to a value that is to be skipped, pour the dye intended for that bucket into the container in its place. (The unused dye may be discarded or may be used for direct, mottled, or tie-dyeing.)

7. Follow Steps 7 through 10 for the "Nine-Step Immersion-Dyed Gradated Sequence" on page 9.

Directions for Direct Dyeing

The direct application of dye onto prepared fabric is a simple and easy way to dye your own fabric. This random application of dye produces an array of spectacular, "accidental" designs, textures, and colors. There is no limit to the variety of designs you can produce.

This technique requires no artistic talent or special tools. Dye is poured, spattered, spooned, sponged, or sprayed onto the fabric. These unusual single- or multicolored patterned fabrics can be used to give a unique designer touch to clothing, accessories, appliqué projects, and quilts.

A WORD ABOUT COLOR MIXING IN DIRECT DYEING

In the direct dyeing process, color mixing occurs when colors meet and blend together. This can create exciting new colors, neutral colors, or muddy colors. Some pieces of fabric may turn out to be less attractive than you had expected. To the untrained eye, some of these could even be called "ugly." Do not throw them away! They are just waiting for the right companion fabric to make a spectacular quilt or garment. *The Uglies* wall quilt pictured and described in Chapter 5 shows examples of such fabrics and how they can be used.

SUPPLIES NEEDED

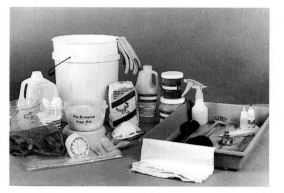

1-2 Supplies required for direct dyeing.

One plastic bucket for presoak solution

1/4-yard to 1/2-yard lengths of 100% cotton, silk, or viscous rayon

Procion MX fiber-reactive dye

Synthrapol SP

Noniodized salt

Dye activator or soda ash

Plastic or glass measuring cups

Plastic drop cloth or plastic sheets such as garbage bags or dry-cleaner bags

Plastic bags such as plastic grocery bags

Plastic measuring spoons

Plastic spoons for stirring and mixing

Plastic cups

Rubber kitchen gloves

Old clothes, old shoes, and an apron

Dust mask

Utensils for dye application: spray and squirt bottles, syringes, toothbrush, sponge, and anything else you might want to experiment with to apply the dye solution

Dyeing Process

Please read pages 1–4 ("Overview of Dyeing Techniques" through "Safety Considerations") and all the steps that follow before starting.

1. PRESCOUR FABRIC: Machine-wash the fabric on the hot cycle with 1 teaspoon Synthrapol SP and 1 teaspoon dye activator per 3 yards of fabric. Fabric may be dried in the dryer and stored for later dyeing, or it may be immediately placed in the soaking solution.

2. PRESOAK FABRIC: Put on rubber gloves and a dust mask. In a 2- to 5-gallon plastic bucket, dissolve 1 cup of dye activator (or soda ash) and ½ cup of salt in 1 gallon of hot water. Soak prescoured fabric (either wet or dry) in this solution for at least 30 minutes or up to 24 hours. The soaking solution can be reused and will keep for months in a covered container. *Be sure to label the container and keep it out of reach of children and pets.*

You can apply dye to wet, damp, or dry fabric. Experiment to find the look that is most suited to your needs. If you wish to apply dye to dry fabric, air-dry the presoaked fabric rather than drying it in your dryer: the alkali from the presoak solution cannot be removed from the dryer, and it will get onto subsequent laundry and may cause skin irritation.

3. MIX THE DYE: Select several dye colors and mix them according to the Dye-to-Water color-value chart. Start by dissolving the amount of dye powder indicated in the chart in 1 or 2 teaspoons of warm water (70°F to 105°F). Stir until all the powder is dissolved and a paste is formed. Add more water if the paste is too thick. Add enough water to this paste to make ½ cup of dye solution. If you are dyeing more than a few pieces of fabric, double the amount of dye powder and water to make 1 cup of the dye solution. You may now remove your dust mask, but continue to wear your gloves until you have finished the dyeing process.

DYE-TO-WATER PROPORTIONS FOR VARIOUS COLOR VALUES

Value	Proportions
light	½ teaspoon dye powder to ½ cup water
medium	1 teaspoon dye powder to ½ cup water
dark	2 teaspoons dye powder to ½ cup water

4. CREATE YOUR DESIGN: If working on wet fabric, wring the fabric out before you begin. Spread the fabric (wet, damp, or dry) out on a flat surface that has been covered with plastic or place the fabric in a large plastic tray. Pour, spatter, spray, or squirt the dye onto the fabric. Add more water to some of the dye solutions to produce lighter values. Mix the dye solutions to produce new colors. The fabric can be flat, slightly scrunched, or folded and tied as for tie dyeing. The more you experiment, the more interesting will be the designs you create. Remember, there is no piece of fabric that you can't use!

5. CURE FABRIC: Cover your finished "work of art" with plastic, or put it in a plastic bag to keep it from drying out. Let the fabric cure for 3–24 hours.

6. RINSE: After the fabric has cured, thoroughly rinse the dyed fabric in warm water to remove excess dye.

7. AFTERWASH: Machine-wash the fabric on the hot cycle using 2 tablespoons of Synthrapol SP, which allows just-dyed fabrics to be washed together. They will not exchange dye at this point. Then machine-dry.

DIRECT-DYEING DESIGN EXPERIMENTS

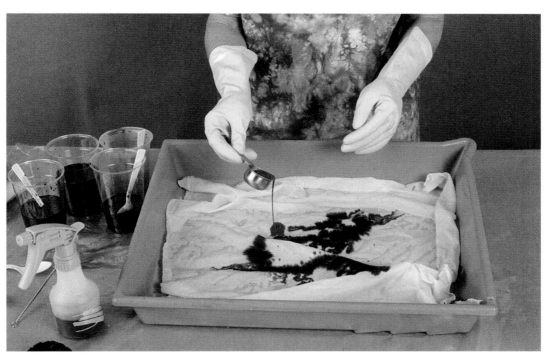

Dye is being applied to the damp pretreated fabric. Because the fabric is damp,
the dye runs across the fabric in unpredictable ways.

Try these simple techniques to create your own unique fabric:

♦ Pour or spoon several colors of dye onto your fabric in a random manner. You may cover the entire piece of fabric with dye, or you may let some of the background fabric show. To create sky fabric, dilute the dye solution with more water for medium-to-light sky colors. Pour on the dye solution, leaving as much white space as necessary to create clouds.

♦ Dip a sponge into the dye solution. Sponge the dye onto wet, damp, or dry fabric. Experiment to see what you like best.

♦ Pour the dye solution into a spray bottle and spray the dye onto the fabric. Fold or scrunch the fabric and spray from one direction; then refold and spray from a different direction. You can use a single color or work with several colors of dye solution.

♦ Dip a long-handled plastic utility brush or a toothbrush into the dye solution. Hold the brush over the fabric and tap the brush lightly to sprinkle droplets of dye onto the cloth. The size of the droplets is determined by how much dye is on the brush and whether the fabric is wet, damp, or dry.

Leftover Dye

When your fabric dyeing is over for the day, you will probably still have some small quantities of unused liquid dye. As long as the dye has not been mixed with dye activator or soda ash, it can be stored in the refrigerator for several weeks in a covered container. **Label the container clearly, and keep it out of reach of children and pets.** Leftover dye can be used for direct dyeing, or you can use it to create neutral fabrics, as explained below.

USING LEFTOVER DYE TO CREATE NEUTRAL FABRIC

You can create interesting neutral fabric for your quilts using leftover dye from other dyeing projects. The results of this method are unpredictable, but that's half the fun. The final color of your dyed fabric depends, of course, on the specific colors in your mixture of leftovers. The technique is very simple.

Dyeing Process

1. Soak some ¼- to ½-yard pieces of fabric in the soaking solution used for the direct dyeing procedure.

2. Pour all your leftover dye into one container. The resulting mixture is often a mud-brown neutral color.

3. Wring out one of the pieces of presoaked fabric, lay it in a pail or plastic container, and pour dye all over it. Make sure to cover all of the fabric by moving it around in the dye; however,

These fantastic fabrics were dyed using the direct dyeing procedure.
There are light sky colors as well as very dark accent fabrics.

don't work the dye into the fabric to a great extent. If you just pour the dye onto the fabric and move the dye around, you should get an uneven mottled color. (Note that if you want very distinct mottling, you should *not* try to cover all the fabric.)

4. Lift the fabric out of the dye and let the dye drip back into the container. After most of the excess dye has drained, put the fabric in a plastic bag to cure as usual.

5. Add ½ cup of water to the remaining dye. Check the color value of the dye by dipping the corner of a white paper towel into the dye solution. You want to get a distinctly lighter shade than the first color. If the color does not appear to be much lighter, add more water in ¼-cup increments. Once you have the lighter shade you desire, dye the next piece of fabric in the same manner as the previous piece.

6. For the remaining dye, add at least another ½ cup of water. You want a very light shade for the last piece of fabric, so add additional water if necessary.

The *Spring Is Here* wall quilt in Chapter 5 shows this neutral fabric used as a background for appliqué blocks and as sashing between the blocks (see detail below). These neutral fabrics can also be painted with fabric paints to create a patterned fabric.

Detail of the *Spring Is Here* quilt.

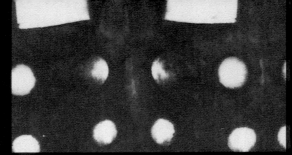

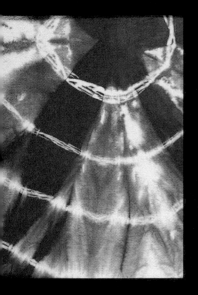
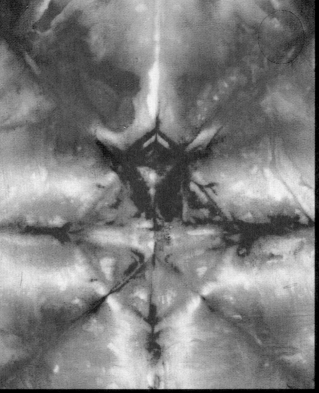

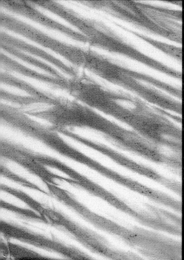
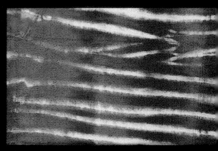
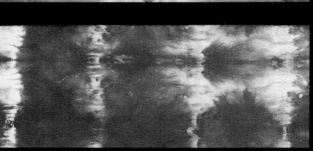

Tie-dyed fabrics that can be used in quilts and "wearable art" projects.

TIE DYEING AND SHIBORI-WRAP DYEING

*Tie dyeing and shibori-wrap dyeing are forms of the dye-resist process.
In this process your piece of fabric is tied, bound with string or rubber bands,
clamped between pieces of wood, or stitched with thread before the fabric is dyed.
Such methods of resist (stopping dye penetration) allow you to create patterned
fabrics for use in your quilts. You can use either the immersion dyeing method
or the direct dyeing method to create patterned tie-dye and shibori fabrics.
The actual dyeing process is exactly the same as described in Chapter 1,
except that in tie dyeing and shibori-wrap dyeing, the fabric
does not remain flat. Instead, it is manipulated prior to
being dyed, as described in the experiments below.*

**Be sure to read all of the relevant dyeing instructions in Chapter 1
before trying any of the dyeing experiments presented in this chapter.**

Most of the techniques we present produce somewhat random results despite the fact that specific folding directions are given. Especially with the direct dyeing method, dyes tend to run or wick into different areas and colors blend together in somewhat unpredictable ways. The final results are often surprising, but usually pleasingly so.

Tie Dyeing

Read the "General Notes" that follow and then select some of the tie-dye experiments to try. Each experiment results in a different type of patterned fabric suitable for your quilts or wearable art projects. Depending on the dyeing method selected, the fabric is presoaked in water or soda ash solution once it has been bound. Refer to "Dyeing Shibori-Wrapped and Tie-Dyed Fabric" on page 29 for instructions on dyeing the fabric.

GENERAL NOTES

Prescour and dry your fabric as directed in Chapter 1 (see pages 5–6). Cut the fabric into the size pieces you want. Most of the time an 18" x 15" (or so) piece of 45"-wide fabric works well because you can do a lot of experiments without using up massive amounts of yardage. Also, it does not take a long time to bind off or stitch the fabric in preparation for dyeing when it is this size. Note that if you bind large pieces of fabric, you will have many thicknesses of fabric in the bundle; the dye will not penetrate to the inside fabric, resulting in a large section of undesigned fabric.

When removing your rubber band bindings, be careful not to lose the bands down the drain. If you cut the bands off, be very careful not to cut a hole in the fabric.

SUPPLIES NEEDED

The supplies needed for these experiments are the same as for the immersion and direct dyeing methods (see pages 5 and 11). In the tie-dyeing process you are simply binding, clamping, or stitching your fabric prior to actually dyeing it. For the specific resist techniques covered in this chapter, you will need the following items:

Package of rubber bands

Four or five small aluminum C-clamps (available at hardware stores)

Thin varnished pieces of wood about 2" square

A few pennies or other coins

Small nylon net bag about 5" x 8"

Needle and a spool of button and carpet thread

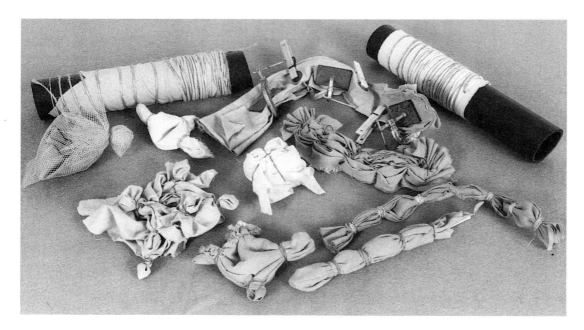

2-1 The fabric as it looks once it has been manipulated and secured. It is now ready to be dyed.

Tie-Dye Experiments

CENTRAL PINCH

Lay the fabric flat. Grab the center of the fabric and pull it up so the fabric drapes downward (Fig. 2-2). Secure this fabric tube loosely at 1½" intervals with rubber bands (Fig. 2-3).

You will learn from experience how tightly to wrap the rubber bands. A 1½"-diameter rubber band can usually be wrapped around the cloth four or five times. If it is wrapped too tightly, however, no dye will reach the center layers of fabric, and that section will have no color and therefore no pattern.

The fabric can also be draped over a plastic pole about ½" to 1" in diameter. In this case, secure the bundle around the plastic pole at 1-½" intervals with rubber bands.

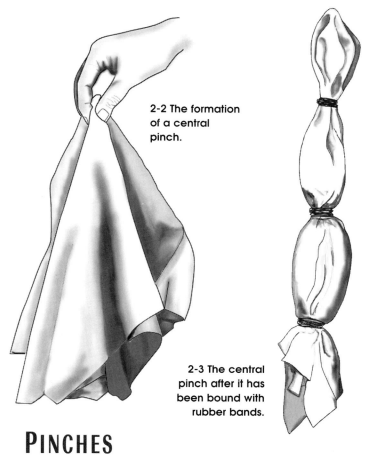

2-2 The formation of a central pinch.

2-3 The central pinch after it has been bound with rubber bands.

PINCHES

Lay the fabric flat. Then pinch up a 1" piece of fabric. Secure the pinch at its base with a rubber band (Fig. 2-4). (Note that a wide rubber band will produce a slightly different look than a narrow rubber band.) Make sure the rubber band is tight. Make as many of these pinches as you want. The fabric can be dyed all one color using the immersion method, or you can use the direct-dye method and spoon or drop the dye on the presoaked fabric. The tips can be dyed one color and the unpinched fabric can be dyed a different color.

2-4 A piece of fabric prepared with small pinches.

CRUNCH IN A NYLON BAG

This technique gives the fabric a mottled appearance. To begin, sew a 5" x 8" bag from nylon net or use a nylon net bag such as the kind that toys come in or flower bulbs are shipped in. Stuff your piece of fabric into this bag and close the top of the bag with a rubber band (Fig. 2-5). Carefully pull on the fabric in the bag to loosen it a little so the dye will be able to penetrate. The more tightly the fabric is stuffed into the bag, the more pronounced will be the mottling because less dye will be able to penetrate to the center of the fabric ball. You can experiment with different degrees of compactness of the fabric ball to determine which final results you prefer. This technique works very well with immersion dyeing.

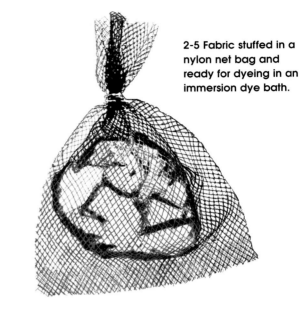

2-5 Fabric stuffed in a nylon net bag and ready for dyeing in an immersion dye bath.

ACCORDION PLEAT

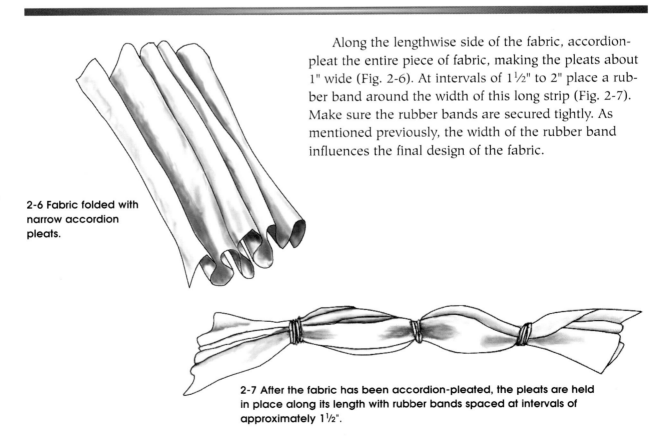

Along the lengthwise side of the fabric, accordion-pleat the entire piece of fabric, making the pleats about 1" wide (Fig. 2-6). At intervals of 1½" to 2" place a rubber band around the width of this long strip (Fig. 2-7). Make sure the rubber bands are secured tightly. As mentioned previously, the width of the rubber band influences the final design of the fabric.

2-6 Fabric folded with narrow accordion pleats.

2-7 After the fabric has been accordion-pleated, the pleats are held in place along its length with rubber bands spaced at intervals of approximately 1½".

FLAG FOLD

This technique works best with the direct dyeing method, using several colors of dye on the folded fabric. Fold your fabric in thirds along the lengthwise side (Fig. 2-8). Then flag-fold this strip of fabric (Fig. 2-9). Your resulting piece of fabric will be a triangle (Fig. 2-10). Bind off the corners of this triangle with rubber bands. The bands should be about 1" from the tips

(Fig. 2-11). Spoon one color of dye onto the tips of the corners, and pour a different color of dye on the rest of the fabric. Another way to dye the fabric is to color the tips one color, the folds a second color, and the rest of the fabric a third color.

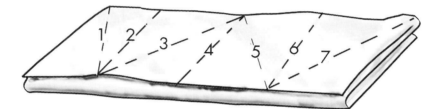

2-8 Fabric folded lengthwise in thirds.

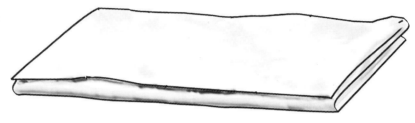

2-9 Follow the numbered sequence to flag-fold the pleated fabric.

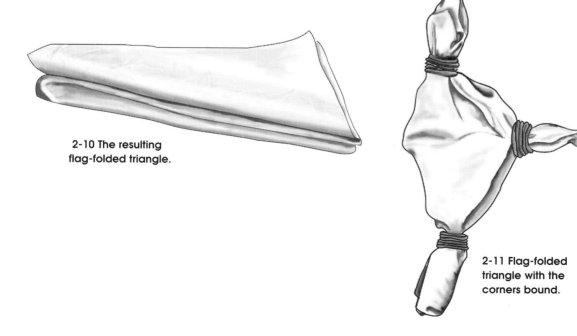

2-10 The resulting flag-folded triangle.

2-11 Flag-folded triangle with the corners bound.

FOLDED SQUARES

Direct dyeing is the best method for this technique if you want to create a multicolored fabric. Fold the fabric in thirds along the lengthwise side (Fig. 2-8) as in the flag-fold technique above. Then fold the fabric into squares (Figs. 2-12 and 2-13). Bind off the four corners as in the flag-fold method (Fig. 2-14). Dye the corners one color and the rest of the square another color. Three colors of dye work nicely in this method also. Use different colors for the corners, folds, and center.

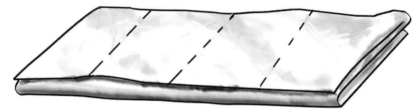

2-12 Fold along the dotted lines to create a square.

2-13 The folded square. Depending on the original size of your piece of fabric, you might end up with a rectangle.

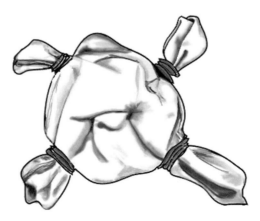

2-14 The folded square or rectangle with the corners bound.

CLAMPS

Fold the fabric lengthwise into fourths. Use thin pieces of plastic or thin varnished pieces of wood for this technique. Put a piece of wood on the top surface of the fabric and another directly underneath it. Hold the wood securely with a small aluminum C-clamp twisted tightly in place (aluminum won't rust and stain the fabric). Place several of these pieces of wood and clamps along the fabric in any pattern you desire. Then take two pennies and place one on the top of the fabric and one directly underneath the fabric bundle and hold them in place with a plastic clothespin. Do this in any pattern you wish on the fabric (Fig. 2-15). Then use the immersion dyeing method to dye the fabric.

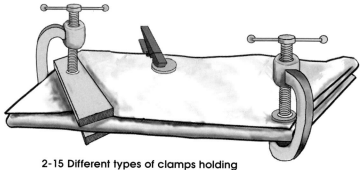

2-15 Different types of clamps holding wood and coins in place on the fabric.

Wherever you have clamped a coin or wood the fabric will remain undyed. After you have completed the dyeing process and rinsed, washed, and dried the fabric, you can use a sponge to color the undyed places with fabric paints. This adds a second color to the fabric.

SWIRL IN A BALL

Lay the fabric flat. Pinch a small bit of the fabric at the center. While holding onto this pinch, twist the remaining fabric clockwise into a ball (Fig. 2-16). Secure this ball with rubber bands so that it is divided into quarters (Fig. 2-17). The bands must hold the ball in place but not be so tight that they prevent the dye from penetrating. For a single color, the immersion dye method is most suitable. Two colors can be used if you follow the direct-dye procedure, alternating the colors in the four quarters. Remember to turn the ball over and dye the bottom.

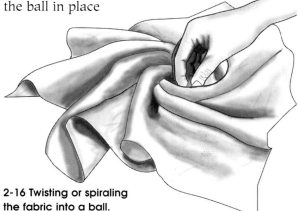

2-16 Twisting or spiraling the fabric into a ball.

2-17 The fabric secured into a ball with rubber bands. Note that the bands divide the ball into quarters.

STITCH RESISTS

Lay the fabric flat. Take a heavy thread such as button and carpet thread and with long basting stitches stitch parallel lines lengthwise across the fabric. Place the lines about 1½" apart. At one end of each line leave a 2" tail of thread, untied (Fig. 2-18). When all the stitching is complete, pull on each thread to gather the fabric tightly (Fig. 2-19). Then tie off the lines of stitching.

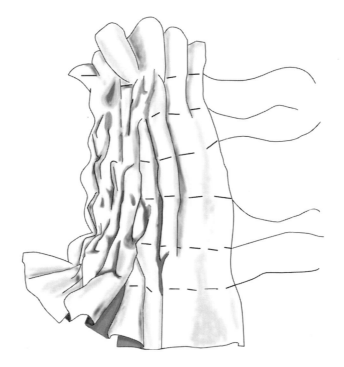

2-18 Large basting stitches sewn in several rows across the length of a piece of fabric.

2-19 The gathered fabric as it looks once the stitches have been pulled tight.

Shibori-Wrap Dyeing

Shibori dyeing originated in Japan and China. The Japanese have developed very sophisticated variations of this technique. As used in this book, "shibori dyeing" refers to wrapping a length of fabric around a section of PVC pipe. The fabric is wrapped with twine and then pushed together or compressed. The fabric should be dry when being wrapped, then soaked in water for 10 minutes prior to immersion dyeing *or* soaked in presoak solution for 30 minutes before direct dyeing.

After the fabric has been dyed and the twine removed, lovely wavy lines and stripes are part of the fabric design. Variations can be achieved by using thick or thin twine for binding. Whether the string is wound on the pole with even spacing or with crisscrossing lines also influences the pattern created. If the fabric is pushed compactly on the pole, less dye penetrates than if the fabric is pushed together only lightly. Several other variations are listed in this section for you to try.

SUPPLIES NEEDED

One or more pieces of PVC pipe, both ends sanded smooth (see Note below)

Package of rubber bands

Ball of cotton or nylon twine

Note: The PVC pipe we used in these experiments was 2" to 2½" in diameter and about 14" long. This size is easy to control, but you can also obtain rectangular pipe or pipe with a larger diameter in order to do some other interesting experiments.

Shibori Wrapping Techniques

Here are two basic wrap techniques, the diagonal fabric wrap and the horizontal wrap, followed by a series of experiments you can try with either wrap method. When you are ready to

dye your shibori, refer to the directions for "Immersion Dyeing: Mottled and Tie-Dye Variation" on page 7 or the directions under "Direct Dyeing" on page 12.

DIAGONAL FABRIC WRAP

The first step in the shibori method is to determine whether you want to wrap the fabric straight or diagonally onto the pole. The first procedure we show uses fabric that is wrapped diagonally.

Lay the fabric flat and lay the pipe diagonally across the top right-hand corner (Fig. 2-20). Roll the pipe toward you, wrapping all the fabric smoothly around the pipe (Fig. 2-21).

2-20 Placement of the fabric for a diagonal wrap.

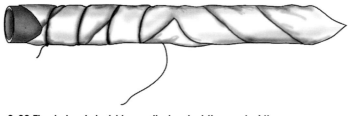

2-21 The fabric wrapped around the PVC pipe.

2-22 The twine is held by a slip knot at the end of the pipe and part of the fabric is wrapped with the twine.

Make a slip knot on the end of a roll of twine. Slip this knot over the end of the fabric on the left end of the pipe, securing it with a rubber band. Wrap the twine around the pipe, spacing the wraps about every ½" (Fig. 2-22). (Once you have seen the pattern produced by the dye you may wish to widen the space between the twine wraps to obtain a different pattern.)

Wrap the fabric for about 4". Then stop and push the wrapped fabric down to the end of the pipe where the wrapping began (Fig. 2-23). Continue wrapping, then stop and push another 4". Continue until you have wrapped and pushed the entire piece of fabric (Fig. 2-24). Cut the twine and secure the end with another rubber band.

2-23 One end of the pipe shows the fabric after it has been pushed down. There is still more fabric to be wrapped with twine and pushed down.

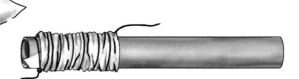

2-24 The fabric has all been wrapped with twine and pushed down to one end of the pole.

HORIZONTAL WRAP

Lay the fabric flat and lay the pipe parallel to one edge of the fabric (Fig. 2-25). Wrap all the fabric onto the pipe and bind and push as in the "Diagonal Fabric Wrap" technique above.

Note: Do not use a piece of fabric larger than 15" x 15" on a pole that is 2½" in diameter. If you do, you will have too many layers of cloth for the dye to penetrate. If you want to dye bigger pieces of fabric, use a larger-diameter pole. Once you have some experience and you understand how the binding works in relation to fabric thickness, you may wish to ignore this note. For instance, you can get a dark and light bind on one piece of fabric by folding it in half when you roll. However, for best results as you are learning this technique, use only smaller pieces of fabric.

2-25 The placement of the pole and fabric for a horizontal shibori wrap.

Shibori Wrapping Experiments

You can do the following experiments using either shibori wrap technique (horizontal or diagonal). Experiment to get the results you find most attractive.

WRAP AND TWIST

Wrap the fabric onto the pole. Wrap the twine around the pole for 4" and push the fabric down. Wrap another 4" with twine, and then, instead of pushing the fabric straight down, twist the fabric counterclockwise as you push. Wrap 4" more with twine and push straight. Then wrap and twist. Continue until you have wrapped all of your fabric with twine and pushed it down. You can vary the spacing to 2" if you wish.

NO-TWINE METHOD

Wrap the fabric around the pole. Secure the fabric onto the pole with a rubber band. Push the fabric down to the end of the pole and secure the other end of the fabric with a rubber band. In this method, compression alone holds the folds in place.

28

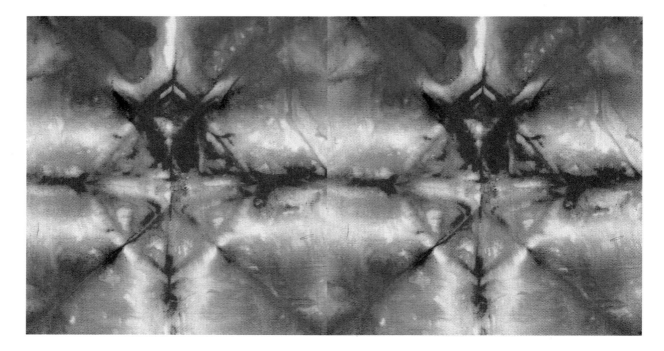

RECTANGULAR PIPE

Use a piece of square or rectangular plastic pipe (for example, downspout) and wrap and bind as in the horizontal-wrap method.

PLEAT AND WRAP

Pleat a piece of fabric with 1" pleats and iron the pleats down. Using a basting stitch on your machine, stitch across both ends and through the middle to hold the pleats in place. Wrap the pleated fabric on your pole and bind with twine as usual.

TWINE MADE FROM SELVAGES

Many sewers and quilters tear the selvages from their fabric before cutting it into pieces. If you do this, save these selvage strips and knot them together. Then you can bind your fabric with these strips instead of twine, and push as usual. This selvage binding is about 1/4" thick so it produces a different shape in the lines than does regular twine.

KNOTTED TWINE

As your binding twine, you can use short pieces of string tied together with knots. The knots provide a resist pattern that is somewhat different from that produced using unknotted twine.

Note: Do not reuse your twine for subsequent dyeings unless you do not mind the possibility of dye transfer from the twine to the new fabric.

PINCH, PLEAT, AND CRUMPLE

In all the previous methods the fabric was wrapped smoothly onto the pipe. However, as you wrap for this method, pinch and pleat bits of fabric under the twine as you wrap the twine down the pipe. Push as in previous methods.

TIE-DYE PINCHES

Make a piece of pinched tie-dye fabric (see page 19). Smooth it out as best you can and wrap and bind it on the pole. Because of the rubber bands and the bulk of the separate pinches, it will not be very flat on the pole.

Dyeing Shibori-Wrapped and Tie-Dyed Fabric

After you have manipulated your fabric with any of the tie-dye and/or shibori techniques, proceed to dye it following the instructions given under "Immersion Dyeing: Mottled and Tie-Dye Variation" (page 7) or "Direct Dyeing" (page 12). Immersion dyeing is usually best if you want only one color on your fabric; direct dye works well for producing multicolor fabrics, but it can also be used to create single-color fabrics. If one dyeing method is preferred over the other for a specific technique, it is noted in the directions.

You may also choose to use the technique outlined under "Immersion Dyeing: Mottled and Tie-Dye Variation" and then overdye the fabric in a second color. After your fabric has been dyed, washed, and dried, just rebind your dyed fabric using a different technique and redye it. You will thus produce a two-colored tie-dye fabric.

The direct-dye technique works very well for smaller pieces of fabric, say, ⅛ to ¼ of a yard. Larger pieces are best dyed using the technique outlined under "Immersion Dyeing: Mottled and Tie-Dye Variation" on page 7. Up to 2 yards (this can be the sum of many smaller pieces) can be dyed at one time in a 1-gallon dye bath using the immersion technique. Therefore, the amount of yardage you want and the number of colors you need will determine which technique you use.

If you are using the immersion dyeing procedure, remember to soak your fabric in plain water prior to dyeing. You can soak your fabric in water, wring it out, and proceed to do your bindings, but we prefer to soak the fabric in the water after it is bound (this approach seems easier and less messy). Allow the fabric to soak for at least 10 minutes so it does get thoroughly wet. Then carefully squeeze or wring out the excess water prior to dyeing.

If you use the direct-dye technique, soak your fabric in the solution of salt, water, and dye activator for 30 minutes just prior to dyeing. Dye activator can be a skin irritant, so it is best not to soak the fabric prior to binding. A large medicine dropper is a good tool to use when applying the dye for the direct-dye method in the shibori or tie-dye techniques. When dyeing the fabric on the PVC pipes (shibori technique), you can place the dye in random blotches all over the fabric, or apply the dye in vertical stripes from the top to the bottom of the pole, or apply the dye in horizontal bands around the circumference of the pole. Each type of dye application will produce a different type of design.

Dye being applied with a medicine dropper to a piece of fabric folded using the flag-fold technique. The red, yellow, and blue fabric in the foreground shows the fabric after it has been dyed.

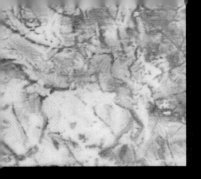

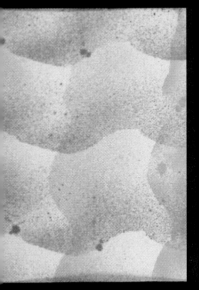
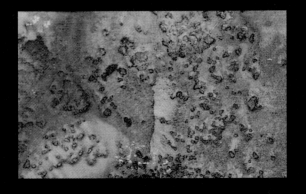
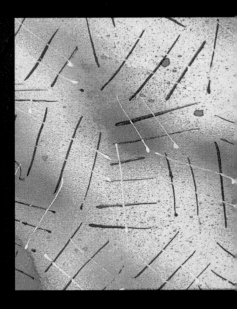

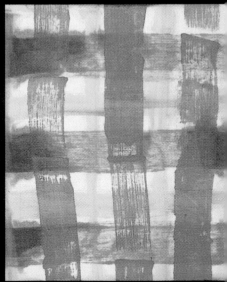
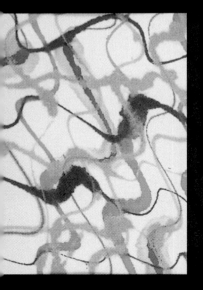
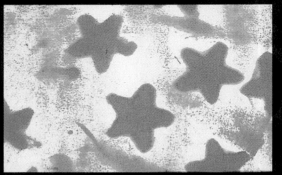
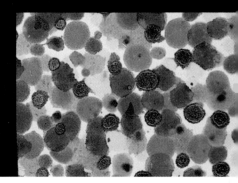

Fabrics created using a variety of fabric-painting techniques.

CHAPTER 3

FABRIC PAINTING

You can have fun making beautiful painted fabric when you follow the easy instructions for the experiments in this chapter. No artistic talent is needed, and even children can do many of the techniques. Fabric painting does not rely on dyeing, although you may choose to paint on some of the fabric you have dyed. Fabric paint is applied directly onto plain or patterned fabric.

Overview of Fabric Painting

There are many types of fabric paints available to help you create exciting fabrics for your quilting projects. Fabric paints are very easy to use, and even children can do many of the techniques. With paints, you do not need any chemicals to achieve a coloring reaction.

Paints are readily available at local art stores, craft outlets, and fabric stores. If you want specialized brands and types that are unavailable locally, you can easily order them from mail-order sources. Note that there is no

perfect brand. Each manufacturer has created special colors of paint, certain special-effect paints, paints of a certain consistency, and so on; and if you have the time and money, it is worthwhile to experiment with many brands to learn which ones work best for the techniques that most appeal to you.

Fabric paints color fabric in a whole different way from dyes. While dye molecules bond with the fiber molecules of a fabric to create the color, fabric paints coat the surface of the fabric. For this reason, paints can alter the feel, or "hand," of the fabric slightly and can cause the fabric to stiffen a bit. (Some brands alter the feel of the fabric very little, while others alter it significantly.) Further, if the paint is applied too heavily, it can crack or peel off.

For coloring large amounts of fabric, paints are definitely more expensive to use than dyes. However, paints can usually be used on both natural and synthetic fibers, which can be very useful to the person creating wearable art: sewers often prefer permanent-press or synthetic fibers in garments. Always be sure to check the instructions on the paint you are using to see what fabrics it can be used on.

Paints can vary in consistency. They can usually be thinned slightly with water, although this may lighten the color somewhat. Some brands of paint have a special extender you can purchase to lighten the color to produce pastel shades. You can also experiment and create new colors by mixing paints.

Paints can be transparent or opaque. Opaque paints can cover darker fabrics, while transparent paints work best on white or very light-colored fabrics. Most paints have to be heat-set. Usually this is accomplished by ironing on the wrong side of the fabric for up to 2 minutes.

In most cases, cleaning up after you use fabric paints is fairly simple. The tools and brushes you use can be cleaned with soap and water, so you do not need to purchase any special solutions.

SPECIAL PAINTS FOR SPECTACULAR EFFECTS

Special-effects paints can create texture and visual glitz that cannot be duplicated with dyes. Some of these types of paint are described below, and Appendix B lists some of the brands of paint you can use to create lovely fabrics for your quilting projects.

PUFF PAINTS

Puff paints are a good example of special-effects paints. When these paints are heat-set on the wrong side, the painted area puffs up and

turns somewhat fuzzy. (Don't apply these paints too thickly, however, or the fabric will pucker.)

METALLIC PAINTS

Metallic paints give the fabric surface an iridescent glow. Note that you can mix metallic pearl white with any regular paint color to achieve a metallic effect, so you can create a variety of metallic colors without having to buy a whole set.

DIMENSIONAL PAINTS

Dimensional paints are sold in bottles with a narrow tip so that the paint can be squeezed out in a fine line. The lines you draw with these paints will be raised off the surface of the fabric. If you wish, you can use dimensional paints as regular fabric paint by squeezing the paint onto your glass surface and smoothing it out before stamping or painting with it.

GLITTER OR SPARKLE PAINTS

In these paints, the colored glitter is suspended in a transparent medium. You can brush or apply the paint directly from the bottle, and once the medium dries clear, you'll have a line or area of glitter that sparkles.

Remember that all colors of paint, like dye, will appear darker when wet. Keep that in mind when you are mixing colors to match other fabric.

PAINTING SUPPLIES

See Appendix A for a list of mail-order sources for fabric paints.

FABRIC

White 100% cotton fabric is a good choice. The paint colors will show up best on white, and it is the fabric of choice for the majority of quilters. Wash and dry the fabric, but *do not use Synthrapol SP or soda ash prescour.* Cut the fabric into pieces about 12" x 12" (for about 9 pieces per yard of 36"-wide fabric) or 11" x 12" (for about 12 pieces per yard of 45"-wide fabric). This size fabric gives you the opportunity to experiment with a variety of techniques and paints without using yards and yards of cloth.

PAINT

Use any colors or brands you wish. If you buy three primary colors, you can practice color mixing.

PLASTIC CUPS AND SPOONS

Assemble a variety of plastic containers and tools for mixing the paint if you want to create new colors.

WORK SURFACE

Select a working surface that is easy to clean, such as a mirror tile, a refrigerator shelf, or glass from a storm door. Just be sure that all exposed edges of the glass are covered with heavy tape so you do not cut yourself. Also, cover the table where you are setting up your workstation with plastic.

MISCELLANEOUS OBJECTS

Use your imagination as you gather objects with which to paint. Some suggestions: old paintbrushes, foam brushes, small spray bottles, sponges, syringes, foam or hard rubber rollers, medicine droppers, rubber erasers, empty spools of thread, a tin can with nail holes in the bottom, a ball of twine, plastic canvas, plastic tops from different types of containers.

FLAT PLASTIC-COVERED SURFACE

Set up a plastic-covered area where you can lay your completed pieces of fabric to dry undisturbed.

CUP OF WATER

Have some water on hand for thinning the paint if it needs it.

OLD CLOTHES AND AN APRON

Have an old rag or paper towels nearby to wipe off your work surface as needed. Wear rubber gloves when doing any of the techniques involving a spray bottle or sponge, because your hands can easily come into contact with the paints using these techniques.

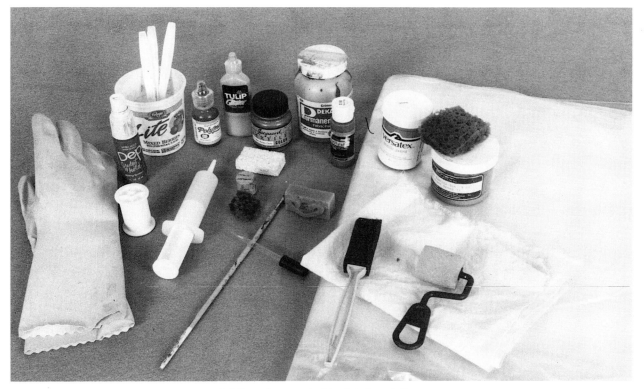

3-1 Supplies needed for fabric painting.

GENERAL DIRECTIONS FOR FABRIC PAINTING

Your fabric may be damp or dry. Note that a particular technique used on damp fabric will yield a different result when used on dry fabric, so be sure to try the techniques you select on both.

Tape the corners of your fabric down on your work surface to keep the fabric from shifting. (With some practice, you may be able to hold down the fabric with your hand and won't need to tape it down.) Spoon the paint onto your glass working surface and use it from there, unless otherwise noted in the instructions.

Painting Experiments

Most of these techniques generate random designs on the fabric. However, with forethought and an understanding of each technique, you can produce planned designs for specific projects. When using a painted piece in your quilt projects, don't ignore the wrong side of the fabric: its lighter color and more subtle design may be just what you are looking for.

Always be sure to read all of the directions before starting one of the experiments.

color to dry before applying the second color if you do not mind a blending of colors.

Cut the sponge into distinct shapes to produce a patterned fabric. Basic geometric shapes such as triangles and rectangles are easy to cut. You could also trace the outline of a simple cookie cutter, a leaf, or some other interesting object onto the sponge and then cut along the traced lines.

SPONGE

Either natural or man-made sponges may be used. In fact, a chunk of foam rubber also works well for this technique. Place a teaspoon of fabric paint on your glass surface. Dab the sponge in the paint and then dab it a couple times on the glass surface to remove lumps of paint and distribute the paint evenly on the sponge. Stamp lightly on your fabric at first to determine what value (lightness or darkness) of the color you want to produce. You can always stamp with more pressure to achieve a darker or heavier color. You should be able to stamp several times before you have to reload the sponge.

On the dry fabric, the texture of the sponge will show up clearly. When the fabric is damp, the texture will be much more subtle. Try sponging more than one color of paint on a piece of fabric. You do not need to wait for the first paint

SPRAY BOTTLE

Use smaller spray bottles such as those found in the cosmetic departments of discount stores. Some types of fabric paint will have to be thinned with water before they can be sprayed. Be sure the paint has a smooth consistency; lumps of paint will clog the spraying mechanism. Deka Silk does not have to be thinned, nor do any of the paints made for airbrushes. (A spray bottle is a poor man's airbrush!)

Pin the fabric to a piece of cardboard so you can spray straight onto the fabric. *This project is best done outdoors.* Test the nature of the spray on paper first because the spray can be unpredictable. Often it is best to hold the spray bottle about 10" away from the fabric. Cover the entire surface of the fabric with the spray design to produce a mottled-texture fabric. If your fabric is damp, all the dots will be diffused.

The spray bottle also can be used with tem-

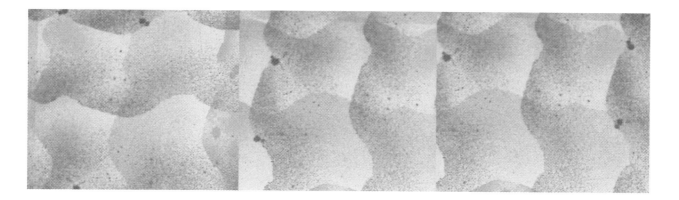

plates or stencils. Spray over the open area of a stencil to color the fabric with the stencil motif, or lay a cardboard template on the fabric and spray paint over it to color the outside edges of the cardboard shape.

Here are some suggestions for creating a specific wavy design using the spray bottle: Pin or tape a piece of fabric to a piece of cardboard. Take a piece of cardboard that is as long as your piece of fabric and about 4" wide and cut some waves across it. Hold this with one hand against your pinned piece of fabric and spray your paint across the wavy line. Move the cardboard down a couple of inches and spray across the wavy line again. Repeat this for the length of the fabric. The fabric can then be turned 90 degrees and wavy lines can be sprayed down the length again. Change colors if you wish. Wipe off the cardboard frequently to prevent drops of paint on it from running onto the fabric.

FOAM BRUSHES

For this technique it is best to use a thicker paint. The possibilities for creating designs with a foam brush are almost endless. For example, you can stick your brush into the paint and swipe it in curved lines on the fabric. You can let some fabric show through, or have the paints touch one another. (The thicker paint minimizes migration of the paint colors.) You can also let the fabric paint dry before adding an additional color. You can use the flat part of the foam brush for wider swipes or the side of the brush to create narrower lines.

This fabric looks terrific if you add some swipes of one of the glitter or sparkle paints to some of the colors. This can be done in several ways. You can apply the glitter paint directly from the applicator bottle and then take a palette knife, hard piece of plastic, or brush and smooth the paint out into a flat line. Or you can put the paint on your glass surface and paint lines of glitter directly onto the fabric with a brush.

ROLLER

Lay some cut-out cardboard shapes on the work surface. Lay your piece of fabric on top of the shapes. Take a 3" or 4" foam roller and run it through your paint. Cover the entire surface of the roller. Roll it out on the glass to make sure it is coated evenly, then roll it over your fabric. Wherever you have a cardboard shape, the dark color of the paint prints. Some texture of the roller will also probably show. You can use any object with a slight bit of relief to it. Things like paper clips, string, plastic canvas, and pieces of plastic gutter guard work well with this technique.

MEDICINE DROPPER

A large medicine dropper works better than the smaller eyedropper version, but either one can be used. Select your fabric paint and thin it down if necessary (it needs to be like water). Fill the dropper with paint and then squeeze out

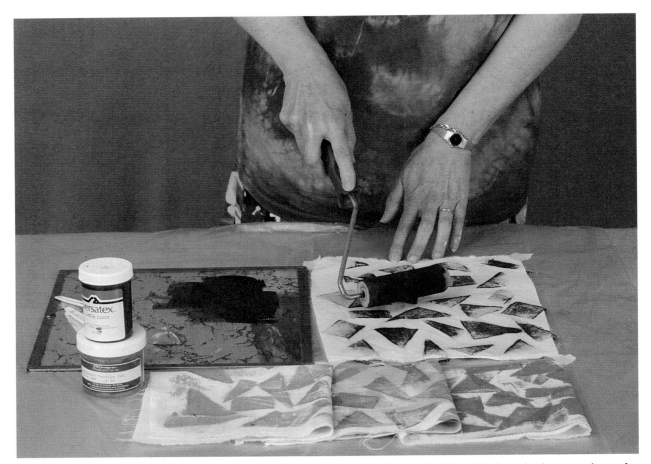

Fabric paint is placed on a glass tile, where the paint is rolled onto a foam roller. The roller is pushed over a piece of fabric, underneath which are triangular shapes cut from corrugated cardboard. The samples in the foreground illustrate the finished product.

drops randomly onto the fabric surface. Change colors to produce a multicolor dotted fabric.

SYRINGE

The paint needs to be as thin as water for this experiment. Remember that the final result will be significantly different if the fabric is wet rather than dry.

Fill your syringe with paint, and paint your design on the fabric. The syringe offers a fair amount of control in terms of the placement of the paint, so you can choose to draw such things as stripes, circles, flower shapes, and random lines. The paints can run into one another and create lovely mixed colors. Do not place complementary colors next to one another or a mud brown color will appear where they mix.

The lovely sunflower fabric shown in the photograph below was made by drawing a sunflower shape freehand with a permanent fineline pen. (We find Pigma brand pens work best.) When this was dry, the flower petals and leaves were filled in with the syringe. The colors migrated out of the pen lines, but this is part of the total effect. A final application of light blue paint was sprayed onto the white background.

PAINTING ON GLASS

This is called monoprinting because you can make only one print from the process. You can use several colors of paint for the design. The easiest way is to take several teaspoons of different colors of paint and place them on top of your glass work surface. Cover an area of the

MIXING COLORS

An understanding of how colors mix is best learned from trial and error. Try some simple combinations at first. For example, make red lines in one direction on your fabric. Then take blue paint and make lines that cross the red ones. Where the red and blue paints mix, you will get a purple color. Any combination of two primary colors will give you a third, equally strong color: red and yellow make orange, while blue and yellow make green. Using complementary colors (colors that are across from each other on the artist's color wheel), such as green and red or yellow and purple (in other words, a combination of all three primary colors), will result in a muddy brown. Buy an artist's color wheel from an art-supply store or perform your own color experiments by combining dabs of paint on a piece of paper.

glass equal to the area of the fabric you will print. Use your finger or a brush to swirl the paint around on the glass to get a pleasing design. Do not mix the colors too much or you will create a glass full of a mud color.

To create a negative design, remove some of the paint from the glass surface by brushing it off with a foam brush. Try not to have any thick ridges of paint standing out on the glass. Carefully lay your piece of fabric over the paint-ed area. Take a hard rubber roller or an old rolling pin and roll the entire piece of fabric until the paint begins to come through the fabric. When you have finished rolling the entire piece of fabric, carefully lift it off the glass and set it aside to dry. (Does this remind you of kindergarten finger-painting fun?) Once you understand the process, you can create more complex, planned designs.

This sunflower design was drawn freehand with a permanent fine-point pen. When dry, the flower petals and leaves were filled in with a syringe.

STAMPING ON FABRIC

All types of objects can be used as stamps. The list of readily available objects includes erasers, jar lids, the end of an empty thread spool, cork bottle-top stoppers, and pieces of Styrofoam. You can cut specific designs into the erasers and Styrofoam or you can just cut simple geometric shapes.

Put some paint on the glass and smooth it out with the back of a plastic spoon. Thicker paint works best. Dip the stamp into the paint. Be careful not to have the paint too thick on the glass or the paint will ooze up the side of your stamp. Stamp the stamp once on the glass to get rid of lumps of paint, then stamp the fabric.

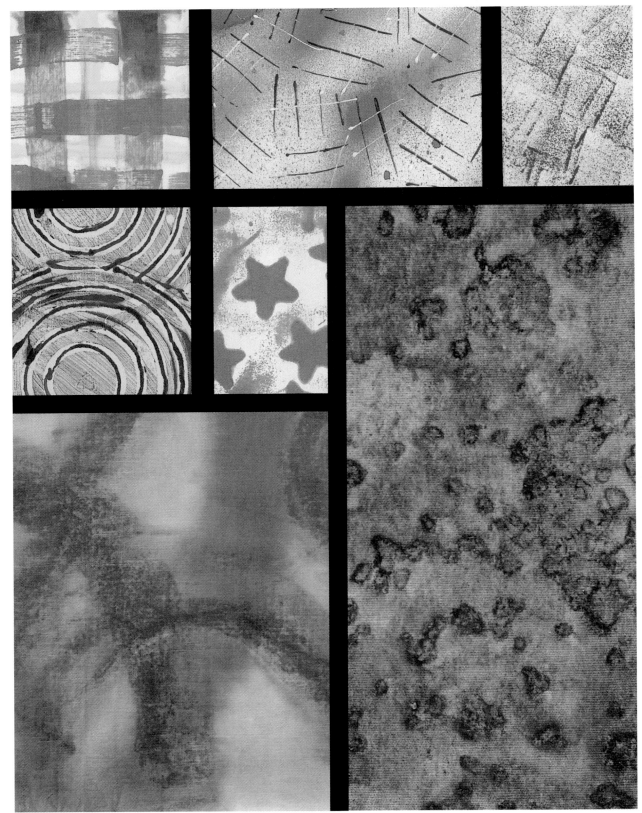

These fabrics were created using the following painting techniques from this chapter:
top left, foam brush; top center, dimensional paint squeezed from a bottle; top right, foam brush;
middle left, stamped circular objects accented with dimensional paint; middle center, roller with star cutouts;
middle right, salt crystals; bottom left, foam brush swirled on wet fabric.

Redip and keep repeating the process. You can stamp randomly or in lines. If you stamp on commercial plaid fabric, you can use the fabric to center your stamp accurately. You can also use commercial rubber stamps. If you wish, a small brush can be used to apply the paint to the surface of the stamp instead of dipping the stamp into the paint.

Jar lids offer another exciting fabric design tool. Collect all sizes and shapes, ovals as well as circles. Dip the lid into the paint on your glass. Stamp lid patterns all over the fabric. Next, take a small round eraser and stamp solid circles inside each larger outlined circle.

SALT CRYSTALS

For this technique a very fine grade of cotton (not muslin) is a good choice, and polycotton blends also produce excellent results. However, silk is the very best fabric for this technique. The salt you use needs to be sea salt or rock salt that has larger granules than table salt. The fabric must be very wet. Paint your colors on the fabric with a foam brush. Do not use thick paint. Sprinkle salt on the fabric and let the fabric dry. Wherever there is a salt granule the paint is absorbed, creating a star-burst effect. There can also be color-wash effects. Experiment with the wetness of the fabric and the drying

DON'T FORGET TO HEAT-SET

Almost all fabric paints have to be heat-set after they dry. Follow each manufacturer's recommendation. In most cases home dryers do not get hot enough, so you will have to use your iron on the cotton setting for up to 2 minutes on the wrong side of the fabric. Then let the pieces of fabric rest for 72 hours before washing them.

time of the fabric to determine the salt effect you like best. Often the back of the fabric is very attractive as well.

The most important thing to remember is to have fun with the paints. Experiment! Let children help you. Children do not have preconceived ideas about what will and will not work, and their youthful spontaneity often produces wonderful results.

This is an example of the fabrics that were given to quilters to use in creating the challenge blocks.

CHALLENGE BLOCKS

The quilt blocks highlighted in this chapter demonstrate that dyed or painted fabric—used either alone or combined with commercially printed fabric—gives a contemporary look to traditional quilt blocks. We refer to the blocks in this chapter as "challenge blocks" because we challenged some quilters of various skill levels to create quilt blocks using the types of fabrics discussed throughout this book.

The Challenge

Packets containing two to four pieces of dyed and/or painted fabric were given to the members of several quilt guilds and to other participants. Included in the wide range of fabrics were the following: immersion-dyed solids, mottled solids, tie-dye patterned fabrics, direct-dye patterned fabrics, shibori-patterned fabrics, and painted fabrics. Challenge participants were asked to make a traditional block of their choice that used dyed or painted fabrics in at least half of the pieces in the block. They did not have to use every type of fabric in their packets, and they were encouraged to select purchased fabric to complete their blocks.

TIPS ON USING COMMERCIAL FABRIC

Selecting commercial fabric for use with dyed and painted fabric is mostly a matter of personal choice. However, the fabrics listed on page 42 seem to work particularly well.

Examples of commercial fabrics that can be very successfully combined with hand-dyed and hand-painted fabrics to make fantastic quilts.

- Prints (small, medium, or large) that are not clearly defined or that seem out of focus combine well with most dyed and painted fabrics.

- Floral and scenic prints that fit this description also work well.

- Atmospheric prints featuring sky, water, or landscape designs are a good choice, giving depth and perspective to your quilts.

- Other good fabric choices include abstract designs, ethnic prints, marbled and feather prints, and geometric prints, especially prints with random dots, swirls, and spirals.

- Plaids, especially madras plaids, also are good choices.

GETTING STARTED

If you have been hesitant to use hand-dyed or hand-painted fabric in your quilts, these challenge blocks will provide you with many ideas. Challenge yourself to make single blocks using dyed or painted fabric. You may choose to use only dyed fabric or only painted fabric, or you may select a combination of dyed and painted fabric and commercial fabric. Even a small amount of dyed or painted fabric can be enough to add an exciting accent to a block.

Start with several pieces of dyed or painted fabric. Look through your fabric collection for fabrics that work well with the dyed or painted fabrics, or go to your favorite fabric store to find coordinating fabrics. As the challenge blocks that follow demonstrate, plaid, floral, and calico fabric can be successfully combined with dyed or painted fabric. Experiment! Be creative! If your block is visually pleasing to you, then you have been successful in your fabric choice.

The first eight challenge blocks show the same basic block, the Four-X block. Since the same quilt design was used in all eight blocks, the different appearance of each block is a function of fabric and color choice. The first block (p. 43, top row, left) has no dyed or painted fabrics in it. It uses only commercial calico and solid-color fabrics. The other blocks in this series use a range of commercial fabrics — prints, ethnic motifs, madras plaid, batik, and reproduction prints — *combined with* various types of dyed and painted fabrics. Notice the range of effects achieved with the various combinations. There are probably fabrics in your fabric collection just waiting to be combined in similar ways.

The rest of the challenge blocks illustrate many ways dyed and/or painted fabrics can be used by quilters in their favorite quilt blocks. The results are spectacular. Study the color and fabric choices carefully for ideas you can use in your quilts. Be sure to read the descriptions of the types of fabrics used in the blocks. These descriptions provide additional information on dyeing and painting techniques you can use as you create your own blocks.

Challenge Blocks

Cynthia Myerberg, Morgantown, West Virginia

This traditional quilt block is made up of purchased traditional solid-colored and calico fabrics. Compare this block with the blocks that contain dyed or painted fabric.

Cynthia Myerberg, Morgantown, West Virginia

Solid colors of crunched and mottled immersion-dyed fabric give this star a reason to glow.

Joyce Mori, Morgantown, West Virginia

The painted fabric framing the central square is stamped with the end of a pencil eraser. The white triangular pieces of fabric are a commercial tone-on-tone that is overpainted with a sponge. The rust is an immersion-dyed solid; the purple center is a dyed mottled fabric. The two leaf prints are commercial fabrics.

Joyce Mori, Morgantown, West Virginia

The center square and its framing triangles are a commercial Native American design fabric. The specific motifs are carefully cut out to create this center design. The darker gray outside fabric is a crunch tie-dye. The red is a solid immersion-dyed piece. The black-and-white fabric is a commercial print.

Cynthia Myerberg, Morgantown, West Virginia

A purchased batik-printed fabric is combined with a medium and a dark value of immersion-dyed terra-cotta fabric.

Cynthia Myerberg, Morgantown, West Virginia

Madras plaid and crunched gold immersion-dyed fabric make a stunning combination in this block.

Joyce Mori, Morgantown, West Virginia

A turquoise, red, and green spatter-painted fabric is used for the center square and the star points. The tiny flower print is a 1930s reproduction print. The navy print is also a commercial fabric.

Cynthia Myerberg, Morgantown, West Virginia

The immersion-dye technique was used to create the apricot solid and the blue crunch-dyed fabric. Unused dye solution from these two dyeings were used along with yellow dye solution to direct-dye the sky fabric. The sky fabric background gives this block a soft, airy look.

Shirley W. Murdock, Roll, Arizonia
Grand Canyon Suite
(from the *Ultimate Book of Quilt Block Patterns,*
by Judy Martin (Crosley-Griffith, 1988))

A green metallic marbled fabric forms the points of the center star. The light patterned fabric is spray-painted with fabric paints. The purple fabric is a dyed solid. The green solid and the black print are commercial fabrics.

Linda Anderson, Morgantown, West Virginia
Sky Rocket (from *101 Patchwork Patterns,*
by Ruby McKim (Dover, 1962))

The rich jewel-tone colors in this block give a regal highlight to the center star sewn from marbled fabric. The dark purple is a mottled solid and the fuchsia is a dyed solid. The dark green around the edges is a commercial fabric.

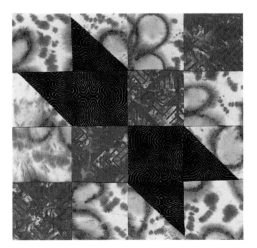

Joyce Mori, Morgantown, West Virginia
Original Design

The light background fabric is direct-dyed in a specific pattern of freehand flowers. Once the fabric is cut up the design becomes unrecognizable. The red and purple fabrics are commercial.

Barb Pavlovic, Morgantown, West Virginia
Ohio Star

The patterned fabric is direct-dyed. The red and blue fabrics are immersion-dyed solids. This favorite block of quilters looks very contemporary done in dyed fabrics.

Pam Kelson, Hants, England
Beach Party

Pat Hill, West Hills, California
Crazy Pieces (from *Scraps Can Be Beautiful*,
by Jan Halgrimson (Weaver-Finch Publications, 1979))

The patterned fabric is colored with fabric paints; Pam carefully placed her templates to achieve the effect of strip-piecing. Just as clear plastic templates can be selectively placed on commercial border and large chintz prints to achieve special effects such as kaleidoscope patterns, so can the technique be used on patterned dyed and painted fabrics. The red is a textured fabric paint. The dark purple is a crunch-dyed fabric. The dark blue fabric is a slightly mottled solid color. The only commercial fabric is the lilac.

A blue shibori fabric frames the center of this block. A dyed purple solid and a mottled dyed red fabric complete this closely related color scheme. The commercial fabric with faces provides a perfect accent for the design.

Kitty Morgan, Morgantown, West Virginia
Churn Dash

Marty Ayersman, Morgantown, West Virginia
Rocky Mountain (from *Quilter's Newsletter Magazine*)

The combination of a cool, blue mottled fabric, a multicolored tie-dyed fabric, and a warm, fuchsia-painted fabric create a luminous effect in this block.

A subtle, split complementary color scheme using solid immersion-dyed mottled fabric and multicolored direct-dyed fabric give this block depth.

Pat Hill, West Hills, California
Hunter's Star Block (from *1001 Patchwork Designs,*
by Maggie Malone (Sterling, 1982))

This block effectively combines marbleized fabric with direct-dyed and immersion-dyed fabric. The results are stunning.

Mary Ellen Andrew, Marseilles, Illinois
Colonial Basket

This block combines a two-color direct-dyed fabric with a salmon crunched-dyed background. The medium values of both hues provide a soft contrast.

Dee Bronson, Hampshire, England
Brotherly Love

"As I looked at the tie-dyed fabric, I saw a man with outstretched arms and decided that he would make an appropriate center for this traditional block," wrote Dee Bronson. Dee has effectively used imagery found in the tie-dye design as the central focus for this block. She combines two crunch-dyed fabrics and a solid purchased fabric with the tie-dyed fabric.

Dianna Parsons, Morgantown, West Virginia
May Basket

A luminous effect is achieved by combining a multicolor high-key direct-dyed fabric with a low-key solid immersion-dyed fabric and a darker blue diffused-print fabric that is purchased.

Jane Fleming, Morgantown, West Virginia
Sweet Heart Garden (from *Best Selling Bazaar Patchwork*, Oxmoor House)

The center of this block is a medium-blue crunch-tie-dyed fabric. The other fabric in the center square is a painted design made by spraying fabric paint (from a spray bottle) over triangular templates. Some metallic paints are used, and the fabric glistens when seen up close. The delicate appliqué rosebuds accent the corners of the block.

Barbara Tomasko, Streator, Illinois
Picture Pretty Pansy

This pansy flower block is perfect for a beginning quilter. All the fabrics are dyed except for the muslin background. The eye is drawn to the lovely shibori-stripe fabric that forms part of the pansy petals. The yellow center is direct-dyed, and the green and red-purple are immersion-dyed solid colors.

Jean Hulslander, Marseilles, Illinois
Colorado Star

This bright and striking block uses a blue painted fabric for the center star, a direct-dyed blue-and-red fabric for the second star, and finally, a bright red suede-like mottled solid fabric for the outer star points, which focus attention back to the center blue star.

Mildred Cramer, Albright, West Virginia
Night and Noon

This block uses a complementary color scheme. The slightly mottled solid navy subtly contrasts with the orange-and-navy tie-dye fabric. A tie-dye orange stripe fabric is used effectively in the corners to focus attention back to the center star.

Millie O'Brien, Morgantown, West Virginia
Weathervane

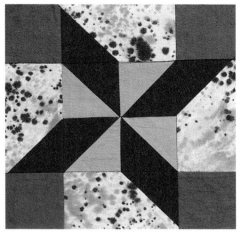

Barb Pavlovic, Morgantown, West Virginia
Clay's Choice

This block makes use of two shibori-stripe fabrics. The stripes are very prominent in the green-and-white fabric, whereas the lilac stripes in the background fabric are barely visible. (Millie dyed the background fabric herself after seeing how much fun it was to dye fabrics!) These pale stripes add some texture to the fabric. They coordinate with the purple crunch-dyed center square and the commercial fabric that is used in the corner blocks.

This primary color scheme would be especially nice for a child's quilt. The spatter-patterned direct-dye fabric was made by dipping a utility brush into the dye solutions and then tapping the brush to sprinkle droplets of dye onto the fabric. The other colors are immersion-dyed solids.

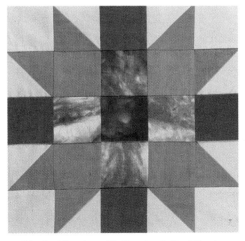

Marty Albertson-Zielke, La Salle, Illinois
Sisters Choice

Janet Simpson, Morgantown, West Virginia
Kaleidoscope

Two values of purple solids are combined with a direct-dyed patterned fabric and a dark green mottled solid in this block. The block has a muslin background.

The printed fabrics are direct-dyed. Janet cut the fabric selectively to get purple patches to place in the diamonds. The solid turquoise fabric and the solid yellow fabric are made using the immersion dyeing process.

Elaine Hutchinson, Morgantown, West Virginia
Turkey Tracks

Nancy Nieslawski, La Salle, Illinois
Rose in Bloom (from *Quiltmaker Magazine*, No. 36)

This red-and-green block could be used in a very contemporary Christmas wall quilt. The green background fabric is presoaked in dye activator solution and then sprinkled with red dye powder (direct-dye method). The second patterned fabric is also direct-dyed. The fuchsia is a dyed solid. Elaine commented that everyone who saw the block in her house liked the way the bright colors worked together.

The center square in this block highlights a tie-dyed circle pattern. Other pieces of this same tie-dyed fabric are used in the corner sections. The mottled triangular pieces are from a fabric made by sprinkling dye powder directly on a presoaked piece of fabric (direct-dye method). A commercial tone-on-tone black fabric and a magenta fabric complete the block.

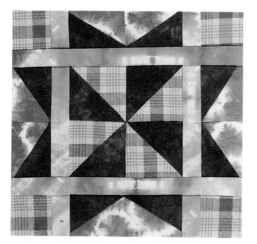

Joyce Mori, Morgantown, West Virginia
Star Lane

Dot Kuffel, Spring Valley, Illinois
Goose in the Pond

A subtle homespun plaid is the only commercial fabric used in this block. The gold and green fabrics are tie-dyed. The rust fabric is a slightly mottled solid color.

All the small dark triangles in this block are cut from the same piece of direct-dyed fabric. The direct-dye method often results in a piece of fabric that has a wide range of colors, making it extremely versatile for quilters. The rust and light green fabrics are immersion-dyed solids.

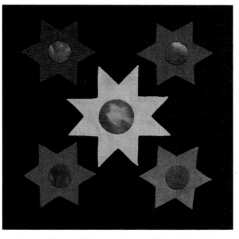

Susan Cook, Morgantown, West Virginia
Stars

Vibrant immersion-dyed solid-color stars with direct-dyed centers seem to float on a background of purchased black fabric. The stark, strong colors give this block an Amish flavor.

Joyce Mori,.Morgantown, West Virginia
The Butterfly

Multicolored direct-dyed shibori-patterned fabric is cut and placed so the lines form concentric squares. The shibori fabric is combined with a light blue crunch-dyed fabric and two commercial prints.

Marty Albertson-Zielke, La Salle, Illinois
Windmill

Vivid painted fabric creates a striking contrast to the solid black background and gives a contemporary look to this traditional block.

Marilyn Wieber, Morgantown, West Virginia
Sky Rocket

A high-value tie-dyed fabric combines with the medium values of the blue and magenta immersion-dyed solid fabrics to add sparkle to this block.

Joyce Mori, Morgantown, West Virginia
Modified Diamond Star

This block uses a light blue sponge-painted background fabric. The multicolored dots are created by dropping fabric paint onto the fabric with a medicine dropper.

Joyce Mori, Morgantown, West Virginia
Octagonal Star

This star comes to life and takes on a contemporary look when subtle homespun plaid is combined with a center pinwheel of red crunch-dyed fabric and a yellow-and-red spattered direct-dye background fabric.

Joyce Mori, Morgantown, West Virginia
Crossroads

The medium-value blue-and-green fabric is a commercial fabric that is placed in a zipper-lock bag which is randomly stitched all over and then immersion-dyed. Where the needle punctures the plastic with holes, the dye can seep into the bag. The design appears as tiny dots of color, occurring in a random pattern as a result of the stitching pattern done with the machine. The fabric surrounding the center plaid square is made by pressing plain fabric on a painted piece of glass. The light blue background and dark blue plaid fabrics are commercial fabrics.

Joyce Mori, Morgantown, West Virginia
Pinwheel

This block demonstrates how a small amount of dyed or painted fabric can be used as a strong accent or focal point in a block. The lovely center pinwheel fabric is an example of what happens when salt crystals are sprinkled on wet painted fabric. The fabric must be wet for the salt-crystal technique to work (see page 39). Joyce combines the painted fabric with a commercially printed sky fabric and a diffused print.

Cynthia Myerberg, Morgantown, West Virginia
Duck and Ducklings

The center square of this block is made up of two commercially printed fabrics, one with random dots and the other with an abstract floral design. Both prints work well with the solid and crunch-dyed fabrics. The red crunch-dyed background fabric was first immersion-dyed in yellow and then crunch-dyed in a fuchsia dye bath.

Suzanne Gainer, Morgantown, West Virginia
West Virginia Lily

Opalescent multicolored tie-dyed fabric combined with a blue tie-dyed fabric, a dark terracotta mottled fabric, and ice blue and light terracotta commercial solid fabrics gives a contemporary appearance to this block.

Helen Cheatham, Grand Ridge, Illinois
Rolling Star

The light blue sky fabric in this block was made by spraying blue fabric paint onto white fabric. Helen combines this fabric with a darker blue direct-dyed fabric, a mottled fuchsia fabric, a commercial floral and geometric print fabric, and a commercial border print fabric.

Cynthia Myerberg, Morgantown, West Virginia
Square Deal

Seven value gradations of immersion-dyed teal fabric create a flow of color from dark to light, creating the glow in the block center. The background fabric is a crunch-dyed fuchsia fabric.

Kathy Venturene, Ottawa, Illinois
Carpenter's Wheel

This exciting block in primary colors combines tie-dyed, crunch-dyed, direct-dyed, spatter-dyed, and mottled fabric with a commercial yellow background.

Kathleen White, Morgantown, West Virginia
Mexican Star

This star block glows with light from the yellow, turquoise, and green direct-dyed fabric that is combined with a mottled turquoise fabric and a violet crunch-dyed fabric.

Dot Kuffel, Spring Valley, Illinois
Strip T's

Tie-dyed fabric, strategically cut and pieced, is combined with a very traditional dark blue calico print in this striking block.

Sylvia Eatherden, Hampshire, England
Castle Wall

The central portion of this block is a tie-dyed fabric that has been cut and pieced to produce a kaleidoscope effect. Other parts of the tie-dyed fabric are used in this block in addition to dark blue and dark violet solid-color commercial fabrics. Primary and secondary colors make this block sizzle.

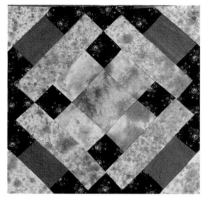

Champaka Seshadri, Morgantown, West Virginia
Album Block

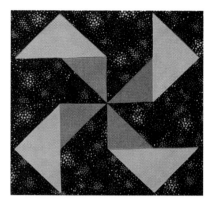

Cynthia Myerberg, Morgantown, West Virginia
See Saw

Black calico fabric is used successfully with brown solid and crunch-dyed fabric and spatter-dyed fabric. The pieces of spatter-dyed fabric are cut from the same piece of cloth. Some of the spatters are small and close together and some are larger splotches of color. Spatter dyeing is an easy way to get several patterns on one piece of cloth.

Adjacent pieces of a light and dark value of the same color (green) make this block seem to fold over like a piece of origami. The black background fabric is a diffused geometric commercial print.

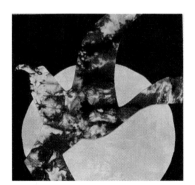

Mary Wilson, Morgantown, West Virginia
Night Moon

Dolly Cupp, Morgantown, West Virginia
Carpenter's Wheel

This original appliquéd block uses an ocher crunch-dyed fabric for the moon. The fabric for the bird is the same crunched ocher fabric crunched again and overdyed in black dye. The black background is a purchased fabric.

Dolly uses a fuchsia and green tie-dyed fabric and green crunch-dyed fabric to make this sizzling block.

56

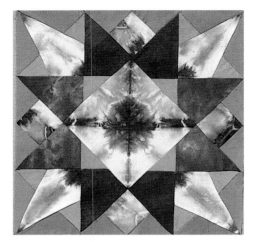

Joyce Dawe, Herts, England
Saturday's Child (from *Scraps, Blocks and Quilts,*
by Judy Martin (Crosley-Griffith, 1990))

The center square and other pieces of this block are strategically cut to take advantage of the colors and patterning of the green and violet tie dyed fabric. Mottled violet and green fabrics and a purchased terra cotta fabric complete the block.

Ruby Sackitt, Morgantown, West Virginia
Flower Basket Block

This block demonstrates how versatile tie-dyed fabric can be. All the flowers and the woven strips on the basket are cut from the same piece of tie-dyed fabric. The basket is a red-violet immersion dyed fabric and the stems are cut from purchased fabric. The motifs are hand and machine appliquéd onto a muslin background.

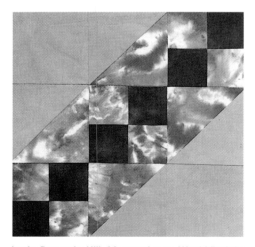

Janie Rexrode Hill, Morgantown, West Virginia
Jacob's Ladder

Janie combines a red-violet and blue-violet direct-dyed fabric with a dark plum and a lavender mottled solid fabric to make this shimmering block.

Vickie Alsene, Ottawa, Illinois
Log Cabin Star

The soft greens in the painted and tie-dyed fabric in the log cabin portions of the block give this block a Southwestern look. The plum fabric that makes up the star is mottled. A purchased white-and-silver fabric with a star motif echo the central star design.

Mary Beth Sands, Ottawa, Illinois
Nine Patch Repeat Variation

Mary Beth combines red and blue calico print fabrics with mottled and tie-dyed fabric to give this block an airy look. The center square in this block is a purchased fabric with a bird motif.

Kristina Potter, Morgantown, West Virginia
Prairie Queen (from *Quilter's Newsletter Magazine*)

The tie-dyed center is the focal point of this block and also dictates the color scheme. A combination of immersion-dyed solid-color fabrics and purchased printed fabrics complete the block.

Pat Read, Putnam, Illinois
Maple Leaf

The rich warm tones of the direct-dyed fabric make this an autumn leaf. Mottled brown and solid green fabrics are used to complete the block. The background fabric is a purchased tan fabric.

Millie O'Brien, Morgantown, West Virginia
54-40 or Fight

Millie's block contains a blue shibori-stripe fabric, a blue crunch-dyed fabric, a peach solid fabric, and a dark-valued direct-dyed fabric that contains all of the above colors.

Helen Ockwig, Yuma, Arizona
Holland Magic

A blue spray-painted fabric forms a pinwheel in the center of this block. A multicolor commercial print is used in four triangles in the design. Two dyed solid colors are chosen to reinforce the colors of the print. Muslin fabric is the background.

Helen Ockwig, Yuma, Arizona
Illinois Star

A commercial beige/white fabric is added to all the other dyed fabrics in this block. The purple and orange fabrics pick up the colors of the lovely direct-dyed mottled fabric. The pale green provides a soothing contrast to the more vivid colors in this motif.

Chris Linten, Morgantown, West Virginia
Snail's Trail

A very subtle blue/green direct dyed fabric is used with a mottled dyed turquoise and a light solid dyed turquoise. A bright dyed yellow solid draws the eye to the corners of the block.

Jeanne Hagan, Morgantown, West Virginia
Weathervane

A multicolor dark direct dye fabric is the focus for this design. A solid purple and blue complete this closely related color scheme. Traditional muslin fabric makes up the background.

Elizabeth Elliot, Ottawa, Illinois
Double X

A mottled gray dyed fabric is paired with a painted stripe fabric and a commercial white-on-white fabric to give this block its cool and quiet appearance.

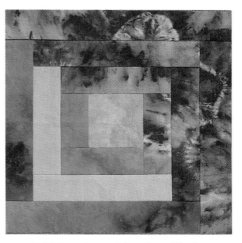

Edith Umphress, Princeton, Illinois
Log Cabin

A brightly colored direct-dyed fabric forms one side of this log cabin. A mottled orange dyed fabric in the center and two shades of turquoise complete the block.

Julie Korba, Ottawa, Illinois
Mexican Star

A commercial plaid, floral print, and muslin fabrics are combined with a dyed gold solid fabric and a direct-dyed mottled fabric.

Evelyn Kelly, Bruceton Mills, West Virginia
Jacob's Ladder

This block glows with excitement. A solid orange dyed fabric complements the direct dye mottled fabric. The black background shows off both these colors to their best advantage.

Edith Umphress, Princeton, Illinois
Patience Corner

All the fabrics in this block are dyed. A tie-dyed fabric is used in the center squares. The orange and medium turquoise are mottled fabrics. The light turquoise is a solid color.

Pat Read, Putnam, Illinois
Cut Glass Dish

A patterned tie-dyed fabric is successfully combined with two dyed solids — turquoise and purple—to create this bright and beautiful block.

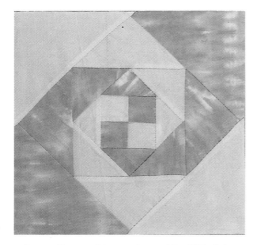

Joyce Royce, Morgantown, West Virginia
Snail's Trail

Both fabrics in this block are dyed — a solid yellow and a blue mottled. These colors give a soft spring look to the block.

Claudette Dale, Morgantown, West Virginia
Cross Bow Tie

Two marbled fabrics combine with dyed brown and purple solid fabric to form the points of interest in this block. The medium purple is a commercial fabric.

Dyed and painted fabrics give a whole new look to traditional quilt blocks.

Dyed and painted fabrics transform traditional designs into contemporary ones in this collage of quilts from Chapter 5.

CHAPTER 5

QUILT PROJECTS

Once you are comfortable with the dyeing and painting techniques described in the previous chapters, you can use these processes to create specific fabrics for your quilting projects. This chapter shows you a range of quilt projects that use dyed and painted fabrics and that are suitable for all skill levels.

Basic Instructions for Quilting

The basic steps of quilting are as follows:

1. Choosing or creating the fabric to be used

2. Cutting the fabric into strips or shapes

3. Piecing the cut fabric into a quilt block or blocks (which may involve appliquéing shapes to the top of the block)

4. Sewing the blocks together (sometimes using sashing between them and borders around them) to create the quilt top

5. Layering the quilt top, the batting, and the backing fabric

6. Quilting these three layers together, either by hand- or machine-stitching or by tying

7. Adding binding to the edge of the quilt to cover the exposed edge

If you are not well versed in these steps, please refer to a basic quilting book, such as *The Complete Book of Machine Quilting, second edition,* by Robbie and Tony Fanning (Chilton, 1994) and *Quilts! Quilts!! Quilts!!!* by Diana McClun and Laura Nownes (The Quilt Digest Press, 1988), or visit your local quilt shop to see if they offer a beginning quilting course.

Quilt Project Instructions

In the projects in this chapter, we give general instructions for creating the blocks but leave finishing the quilt up to you.

We have not included binding or backing measurements. Binding measurements vary greatly depending on how you cut the binding (on the bias or on the grain of the fabric) and whether or not you use a double binding. For backing, try using fabric from your stash or piecing together larger pieces of dyed fabric (not-quite-successful experiments from Chapters 1 through 3 might work well).

We encourage you to add your own personality to our quilt designs. Use dyed or painted fabric where we have used solid, or try a commercial accent fabric as an additional border. Create the design in all dyed fabrics or in a mix of dyed and painted and commercial fabrics. The possibilities are almost endless. A line drawing of each project is included in Appendix D to help you envision some of the possibilities. Just photocopy the drawing several times, and color each copy with various shades and patterns. Try variations of your favorite color schemes, keeping in mind how and where the quilt will be used.

Here are some other tips for using the directions in this chapter.

• Read all directions thoroughly before starting a project.

• Double-check all measurements at each stage of construction, and adjust the border or sashing measurements if necessary.

• Use a ¼" seam allowance on all pieced projects. *The seam allowance is not included in the templates.*

• To create templates for ongoing use, trace each shape from the book onto plastic, add ¼" all around the shape, and then cut the shape out of the plastic. If you're proficient with the rotary cutter, you'll be able to cut many of the pattern shapes without a template.

• When using the templates, remember that a lower-case "**r**" indicates the reverse of the template given. Thus, Cr stands for the reverse of Template C. Simply flip the template over to cut the reverse piece.

• Refer to each project's quilt diagram (Figure 5-1, for example) to see how the pieces are sewn together to create individual blocks and whole quilt tops. The diagram also tells you which fabric is used in each piece of the quilt.

• We used 100% cotton for the fabric in all of these quilts. The dyed fabric in these projects was created from 100% cotton bleached or unbleached muslin or broadcloth that is not permanent press.

DYEING OR BUYING FABRIC TO MATCH

If you are going to combine dyed fabric and commercial fabric in the same quilt, we strongly recommend creating the dyed fabric first and then looking for commercial fabric to match. Trying to dye fabric to match a commercial fabric is difficult, even for the most experienced dyer.

Autumn Glory, 33¹/₂"x 30¹/₂", by Cynthia Myerberg (Morgantown, West Virginia);
machine-pieced, hand-quilted.

AUTUMN GLORY

Autumn Glory is part of a series that Cynthia calls the "Accidental Artist." Some direct-dyed pieces are just too spectacular (purely by accident, in most cases) to be cut into strips or small pieces. Cynthia saw leaf shapes in this piece and chose to treat this work of "art" as a whole-cloth quilt, adding leaf prints created by painting real leaves with fabric paint and printing them onto the fabric.

The sewing skill-level required to make this quilt is beginner, but the surface design possibilities that direct dyeing offers will interest and challenge all levels of quilters.

The directions given will not reproduce the

exact design. However, if you experiment with the various direct-dye techniques, you too may become an "accidental artist."

NAME OF QUILT: *Autumn Glory*

FINISHED QUILT SIZE: 33½" x 30½"

SKILL LEVEL: All levels

FABRIC REQUIREMENTS: Use one fat quarter (18" x 22") of fabric for the center square and approximately ½ yard for borders.

Making the Quilt

1. DYE THE FABRIC: Dye the center square by following Steps 1 through 3 of the direct dyeing process outlined on page 12.

Wring out the presoaked fabric and lay it on a flat surface that has been covered with plastic. Do not smooth out all of the wrinkles because the wrinkled areas sometimes create leaf-like shapes. You may even create some additional wrinkles by pinching up some of the fabric.

Pour a little dye on the wrinkled areas and let it spread for a few minutes. Leave a little space between the dyed area and the next area that you pour dye on. Where the dye colors meet and bleed together, a new color will appear. Continue pouring on the colors of dye until most of the surface is covered. Cover your "work of art" with plastic and allow it to cure for at least 3 hours or up to 24 hours.

Follow Steps 6 and 7 of the direct dyeing process (page 12).

2. MAKE LEAF PRINTS: Paint the veined side of a leaf with fabric paint. Lay the leaf paint-side down on the right side of your fabric. Place a piece of waxed paper over the leaf and gently but firmly roll a rolling pin or brayer over the covered leaf.

3. ADD BORDERS AND EMBELLISH the quilt as desired.

4. QUILT: Cynthia quilted leaf shapes, veins, and stems to emphasize the shapes created by the dye and leaf prints. The parallel lines quilted on the borders are known as channel quilting.

Center Tie-Dye Medallion, 27½" x 27½", by Joyce Mori (Morgantown, West Virginia); machine-pieced, hand-quilted.

CENTER TIE-DYE MEDALLION

The center square of this quilt is a perfect showcase for a piece of special tie-dye fabric or a piece of direct-dyed fabric with an attractive array of colors and patterns.

NAME OF QUILT: *Center Tie-Dye Medallion*

FINISHED SIZE OF QUILT: 27½" x 27½"

SKILL LEVEL: Beginner to Intermediate

FABRIC REQUIREMENTS: The amount of fabric used depends on the size of the center square and the number of borders added. The finished size of the center on this quilt is 12" (meaning we started with a 12½" fabric piece), but we suggest dyeing at least a fat quarter (18" x 22") to allow an interesting center motif to develop. You'll need about ⅛ yard to ¼ yard of fabric for each border. Often much smaller scraps will work. In our quilt, some of the border fabrics are dyed and some are purchased.

Making the Quilt

1. DYE THE FABRIC: Tie dye the fabric for the center square using the flag-fold technique and the direct-dyeing method. You could also use another method of painting or dyeing from

5-1 Piecing diagram for *Center Tie-Dye Medallion.*

Chapters 1 through 3 or find a medallion-like motif in a piece of fabric you've already created.

2. CUT THE FABRIC: Cut a 12½" square that highlights a special area of your dyed fabric. From the border fabric, cut crossgrain strips of varying widths. You will cut them to size as you construct the quilt (see Steps 3 through 5). Our strips measured from 1¼" to 3" wide, resulting in borders ranging from ¾" to 2½" finished size.

3. ATTACH THE MITERED BORDERS: The first set of borders (in our quilt, the yellow and green borders) are mitered. To allow extra length for mitering the corners, cut each border strip the length of the side plus two times the width of the border, plus at least 2" extra.

Center each border along an edge and pin it in place so that the right side of the border faces the right side of the quilt top.

Sew each border from the center point out to the edge, stopping ¼" from the edge, as shown in Figure 5-2. Backstitch at each corner.

Fold the borders open and press them flat. With the quilt wrong side up, draw a line from each corner where the stitching stopped to the nearest outside point where the borders overlap, as shown in Figure 5-3. Then flip the top border underneath the bottom border and mark the second border strip in the same way. At each corner, place the two border strips

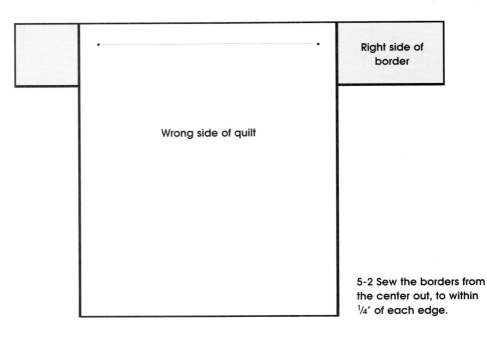

Right side of border

Wrong side of quilt

5-2 Sew the borders from the center out, to within ¼" of each edge.

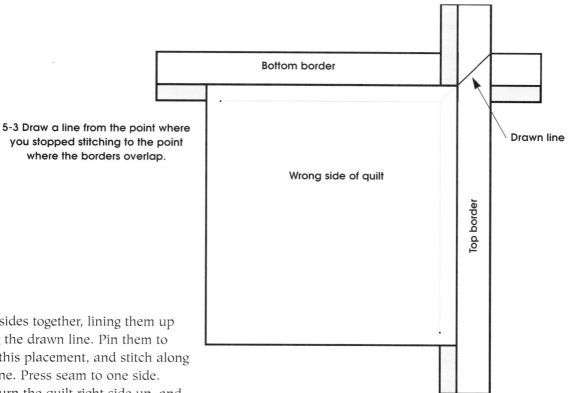

Bottom border

5-3 Draw a line from the point where you stopped stitching to the point where the borders overlap.

Drawn line

Wrong side of quilt

Top border

right sides together, lining them up along the drawn line. Pin them to hold this placement, and stitch along the line. Press seam to one side.

Turn the quilt right side up, and lay the border flat to make sure the miter is accurate. If so, trim off the extra seam allowance. Repeat for the other three corners.

4. ATTACH AND SQUARE OFF ADDITIONAL ANGLED BORDERS: After adding as many mitered borders as you desire, create additional borders by attaching strips of varying widths to each side of the square. We added four additional borders (pale orange, dark multicolor, pale yellow, and medium yellow).

Once you're satisfied with the look of your added strips, rotate the unit so that the center medallion becomes a diamond. This is called *setting the unit on point.* The additional borders are now on the diagonal. To trim the whole unit into a true square, first use a washable marker to draw lines connecting the opposite corners of the center diamond. Square off the corners of the unit by placing a square plastic ruler flush against one of the drawn lines and cutting off the excess fabric, as shown in Figure 5-4. Remember to leave ¼" all the way around to account for seam allowances. Repeat for each edge of the angled borders.

5. ATTACH THE OUTER BORDERS: We added three straight abutted borders to our squared-off medallion. The first two fabrics are dyed (one pale orange, the other bright turquoise), and the outermost border is a commercial fabric.

6. QUILT: Joyce quilted a traditional feather wreath in the center square of this quilt. Note that it can be very difficult to see a quilting design on a highly mottled piece of fabric, and you do not want the quilting to hide or de-emphasize the center piece of fabric that is the focus of the quilt. The borders are channel quilted.

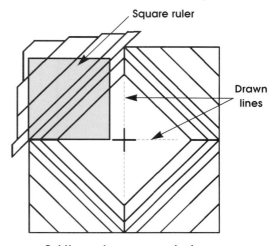

Square ruler

Drawn lines

5-4 Use a clear square ruler to square off the additional borders.

Jane's Colors, 26" x 26", by Cynthia Myerberg (Morgantown, West Virginia);
hand-appliquéd by Cynthia Myerberg and hand-quilted by Jane Fleming (Morgantown, West Virginia).

JANE'S COLORS

A tie-dyed fabric with a sunlit lattice look makes a perfect background for these crunch-dyed tulips. This is an innovative way to use some of your tie-dyed pieces.

Jane Fleming would not let go of this quilt top when Cynthia showed it at the "show and tell" portion of a Country Roads Quilt Guild meeting in Morgantown, West Virginia. It seemed that the colors in the top matched the colors in Jane's new house. A deal was made, and Jane quilted the top to obtain ownership of the quilt.

5-5 Piecing diagram for *Jane's Colors*.

FABRIC KEY

 Green mottled

☐ Plain muslin

▦ Green tie-dyed

⦂ Fuchsia crunch-dyed

NAME OF QUILT: *Jane's Colors*

FINISHED QUILT SIZE: 26" x 26"

SKILL LEVEL: Beginner to Intermediate

FABRIC CHART

Fabric	Yardage
Green mottled dyed	1½ yards
Plain muslin	¼ yard
Green tie-dyed	18½" x 18½"
Fuchsia crunch-dyed	¼ yard

CUTTING CHART

Template or Strip*	Number to Cut	Fabric to Use
Template A	3	Fuchsia crunch-dyed
Template B, Br	3 each	Fuchsia crunch-dyed
Template C, Cr	1 each	Green mottled dyed
Template D, Dr	1 each	Green mottled dyed
6½"-long finished bias strip**	1	Green mottled dyed
12"-long finished bias strip**	1	Green mottled dyed
2" x 24" strip	4	Plain muslin, cut on the crosswise grain
3" x 30" strip	4	Green mottled dyed, cut on the crosswise grain

*Templates are located at the end of the chapter. Remember to add ¼" seam allowance to all templates. Measurements for strips include ¼" seam allowance.

**See instructions in Step 2.

Making the Quilt

1. DYE THE FABRIC: Create the mottled border, leaf, and stem fabric according to the instructions for "Immersion Dyeing: Mottled and Tie-Dye Variation" (page 7), using a green dye bath. Tie dye the lattice background fabric using the folded-square method (page 22) and immersion dye it in the same green dye bath. Prepare the flower fabric using the crunch-in-a-bag tie-dye method (page 20). Then immersion dye it in a fuchsia dye bath.

2. MAKE THE BIAS-STRIP STEMS: Using a plastic, nylon, or metal bias bar is the easiest way to make stems for flowers. Directions included with the bar will tell you how wide to cut a strip to produce a given finished width. After sewing the tube as instructed, slip the bar into the sewn fabric tube, center the seam on the back, iron the tube flat, and remove the bar. The finished bias strip is ready to be cut to whatever length you need.

For the stems in the quilt, make bias strips using a ⅜" or a ½" bias bar and cut them according to the Cutting Chart.

3. CUT THE FABRIC: Use the chart (above) to cut the fabric needed for the quilt.

4. APPLIQUÉ THE TULIP: Appliqué the tulip pieces to the background square in the following order:

Templates C and Cr

Templates D and Dr

Straight stem, curved stem (Use the stem placement guides to position the stems)

Templates B and Br

Template A

5. ADD THE BORDERS: Both borders are mitered. Refer to the instructions in Step 3 of the *Center Tie-Dye Medallion* quilt on page 68. Attach the plain muslin border first and then the green mottled dyed border.

6. QUILT: Jane Fleming quilted in the ditch around the tulips and quilted a feather design in the corners of the plain muslin border. The green border is quilted with a cord-like design created with two rows of curved-line quilting.

Spring Is Here, 28" x 28", by Joyce Mori (Morgantown, West Virginia);
hand-appliquéd, machine-pieced, and hand-quilted.

SPRING IS HERE

The background fabric for this quilt is the neutral fabric described in Chapter 1, pages 14–15. This is an easy appliqué project that combines two commercial prints with hand-dyed fabrics.

NAME OF QUILT: *Spring Is Here*

FINISHED QUILT SIZE: 28" x 28"

SKILL LEVEL: Beginner to Intermediate

FABRIC CHART

Fabric	Amount
Light neutral dyed	Fat quarter (18" x 22")
Dark neutral dyed	⅓ yard
Green wavy commercial print	½ yard*
Beige commercial print	Fat quarter (18" x 22")
Spruce green dyed	10" x 10" scrap
Lime green dyed	Fat quarter (18" x 22")
Purple solid dyed	15" x 15" scrap

*This quilt was bound with the green wavy commercial print. The amount listed above will provide for straight edge binding.

Making the Quilt

1. DYE THE FABRIC: Dye the light and dark neutral fabric according to "Using Leftover Dye to Create Neutral Fabric" on pages 14–15. Dye the spruce green and lime green fabric according to the "Immersion Dyeing: Mottled and Tie-Dye Variation" on page 7. Immersion dye the solid purple fabric, using the mottled variation if you wish.

2. CUT THE FABRIC: Use the following chart.

3. APPLIQUÉ THE STEMS AND SQUARES: To make the short stems, cut four 1¼"-long bias strips from each of the lime green strips (the rest of each strip will be more than enough for the outline squares). Use the placement guide at the end of the chapter and Figure 5-6 to position

CUTTING CHART

Template or Shape*	Number to Cut	Fabric to Use
Template A	16	Green wavy print
	8	Beige print
Template B	4	Dark neutral dyed
	16	Beige print
	4	Green wavy print
Template C	16	Green wavy print
	4	Spruce green dyed
Template D	20	Purple solid dyed
Template E	4	Purple solid dyed
	1	Green wavy print
¼" x 21" finished bias strips**	4	Lime green dyed
11" x 11" square †	4	Light neutral dyed
3½" x 10½" rectangle	4	Dark neutral dyed
3½" x 3½" square	1	Dark neutral dyed
3½" x 3" rectangle	4	Dark neutral dyed

*Templates are located at the end of the chapter. Remember to add ¼" seam allowance to all templates. Measurements for squares and rectangles *include* ¼" seam allowance.

**Create these using a bias bar. See Step 2 of the *Jane's Colors* quilt (page 72) for instructions.

† When your appliqué is complete, trim the squares to 10½" x 10½". Appliqué work tends to draw up the fabric and distort the original size.

5-6 Piecing diagram for *Spring is Here*.

FABRIC KEY

☐ Light neutral dyed		■ Spruce green dyed	
☐ Dark neutral dyed		Purple solid dyed	
▨ Green wavy commercial print		▨ Lime green dyed	
 Beige commercial print			

first the stems and then the outline squares in each light neutral square.

4. APPLIQUÉ THE FLOWER AND LEAF MOTIFS TO THE FOUR BLOCKS: Appliqué the green wavy flower petals and the purple leaves onto the light neutral squares, following Figure 5-6 as needed. Sew the pieces cut from Template E last. Trim the squares to the correct size (10½" x 10½").

5. ADD THE SASHING: Attach a long dark neutral rectangle to each edge of the dark neutral square to create the sashing. Connect the sashing to the light neutral blocks (see Fig. 5-6).

6. APPLIQUÉ THE FINAL FLOWER: Appliqué the four spruce green petals to the center area of the sashing. Appliqué a purple leaf between each petal and a Template E piece in the center of the petals. This is the same flower as that found in the four quilt blocks, except the stems and outline square are omitted and the leaves are placed closer to the center circle.

7. PIECE AND ATTACH THE BORDERS: Piece the borders according to Figure 5-7. Attach the border strips to the edge of the quilt top.

8. QUILT: Joyce outline-quilted the appliqué motifs on the light neutral blocks and then quilted again ¼" from the edge of each motif. Wavy lines were drawn freehand in the sashing strips and were quilted by hand. The remainder of the quilt was quilted in the ditch where desired.

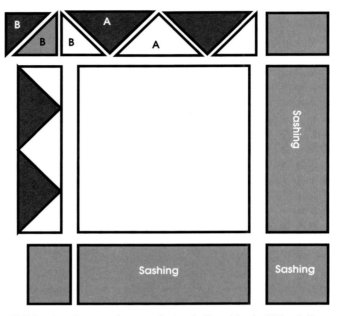

5-7 Border diagram for one *Spring Is Here* block. (Attach the borders after the sashing has been attached to the block.)

Amish Square in a Square, 29" x 29", by Joyce Mori (Morgantown, West Virginia);
machine-pieced, hand-quilted.

AMISH SQUARE IN A SQUARE

The center squares are the focal point for this quilt, and these squares are a shibori-dyed fabric. However, any fabric with visual interest could be substituted. Tie-dye designs would be an excellent choice, for example. Two commercial fabrics were chosen to highlight the dyed fabrics. The colors and design of this wall quilt are somewhat masculine, making it the perfect gift for any man in your life.

NAME OF QUILT: *Amish Square in a Square*

FINISHED QUILT SIZE: 29" x 29"

SKILL LEVEL: Beginner to Intermediate

FABRIC CHART

Fabric	Amount
Shibori-stripe	Fat quarter (18" x 22")
Maroon dyed	Fat quarter (18" x 22")
Turquoise solid dyed	⅔ yard
Rose-beige dyed	Scrap about 8" square
Pink commercial print	8" x 16"
Dark maroon wavy commercial print	½ yard

Making the Quilt

1. DYE THE FABRIC: To create the shibori-stripe fabric, use one of the shibori-wrap techniques in Chapter 2 and then direct dye it with both a turquoise and maroon dye. Create both the maroon dyed and turquoise dyed fabric using the immersion-dye method.

2. CUT THE FABRIC: Use the following chart.

3. PIECE THE BLOCKS: Sew a maroon-dyed A and a shibori-stripe A together. Repeat this 15 times. Form a larger square from four of these units as shown in Figure 5-9. Repeat this three times.

Sew a turquoise border to the top and bottom of each square. Sew a rose-beige square onto each end of the remaining turquoise borders. Sew one of these units to each side of the squares.

Add the wavy-print borders to these squares the same way you sewed on the turquoise borders. Repeat this three times to create Unit 1 (see Fig. 5-9).

4. ADD THE SASHING: Sew a pink print sashing strip between two Unit 1 blocks. Repeat this step with the other two Unit 1 blocks. Sew the maroon wavy-print square between the two remaining sashing strips. Sew this strip between the two sets of squares.

5. QUILT: Quilting lines will not show up against the shibori stripe so it is advisable not to use a fancy motif in this spot. On this quilt, Joyce quilted random wavy lines inside the shibori square to imitate the shibori stripe. She quilted all of the quilt's patchwork pieces in the ditch and used a diamond design in the maroon wavy-print border. Straight-line geometric patterns were used in other areas of the quilt.

CUTTING CHART

Template or Strip*	Number to Cut	Fabric to Use
Template A	16	Shibori-stripe
	16	Maroon dyed
Template B	16	Rose-beige dyed
	1	Maroon wavy print
Template C	16	Turquoise dyed
1½" x 8½" rectangles	16	Turquoise dyed
1½" x 14½" rectangles	4	Pink print
2½" x 10½" rectangles	16	Maroon wavy print

*Templates are located at the end of the chapter. Remember to add ¼" seam allowance to all templates. Measurements for rectangles *include* ¼" seam allowance.

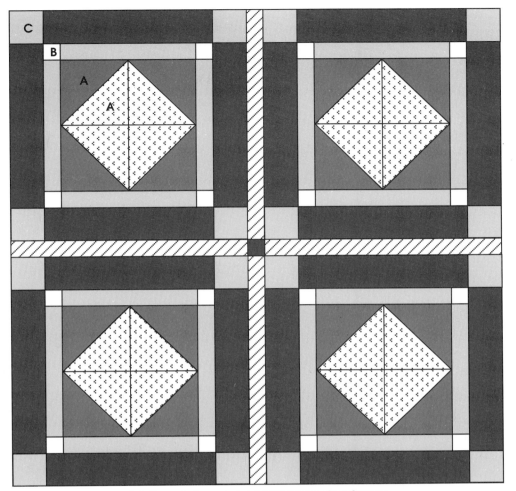

5-8 Overall diagram for *Amish Square in a Square*.

FABRIC KEY

- Maroon and turquoise shibori-stripe
- Maroon dyed
- Turquoise dyed
- Rose-beige dyed
- Maroon wavy commercial print
- Pink commercial print

UNIT 1

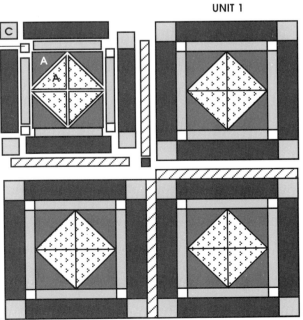

5-9 Piecing diagram for *Amish Square in a Square*.

Who Stepped on the Duck? 34" x 34", by Cynthia Myerberg (Morgantown, West Virginia); machine-pieced by Cynthia Myerberg and hand-quilted by Delores Stemple (Aurora, West Virginia).

WHO STEPPED ON THE DUCK?

Duck's Foot in the Mud (also Bear's Paw) is one of many names for this traditional design. The use of hand-dyed fabrics in the design gives this quilt a contemporary look that sets it apart from its traditional roots. Solid immersion-dyed fabrics, mottled fabrics, and direct-dyed fabrics were used to make this quilt.

NAME OF QUILT: *Who Stepped on the Duck?*

FINISHED QUILT SIZE: 34" x 34"

SKILL LEVEL: Beginner

FABRIC CHART

Fabric	Amount
Blue dyed	1 yard
Blue crunch-dyed	1 yard*
Multicolor spatter-dyed small print	½ yard
Multicolor spatter-dyed large print	½ yard

*This includes enough fabric to make 2½"-wide bias binding for the quilt.

Making the Quilt

1. DYE THE FABRIC: Create the spatter-dyed fabric by using the direct-dye "brush experiment" on page 13 to apply brown, blue, and yellow-gold dye. Varying how heavily you apply the dye will lead to different sizes of spattering. Immersion dye both the solid blue fabric and the crunch-dyed blue fabric (the latter only after crunching it in a bag, as explained on page 20).

5-10 Piecing diagram for *Who Stepped on the Duck?*

FABRIC KEY

■ Blue dyed

□ Multicolor spatter-dyed (large triangles in duck's foot use large print)

 Blue crunch-dyed

CUTTING CHART

Template or Strip*	Number to Cut	Fabric to Use
Template A	64	Small spatter-dyed print
	64	Blue dyed
Template B	16	Large spatter-dyed print
	16	Blue dyed
Template C	25	Blue dyed
Template D	16	Blue dyed
Template E	8	Blue crunch-dyed
2" x 12"	12	Small spatter-dyed print
3½" x 28"	4	Blue dyed

*Templates are located at the end of the chapter. Remember to add ¼" seam allowance to all templates. Measurements for strips *include* ¼" seam allowance.

2. CUT THE FABRIC: Use the chart (above).

3. PIECE THE BLOCKS: Piece 16 duck's foot units (Unit 1) according to Figure 5-11. Piece four duck's-foot blocks (Unit 2) according to Figure 5-12.

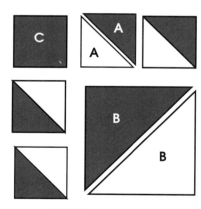
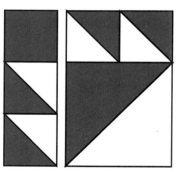
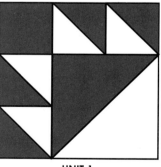

5-11 Piecing diagram for Unit 1 of *Who Stepped on the Duck?*

UNIT 1

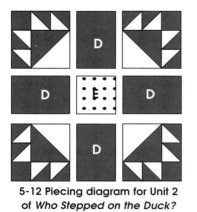

**5-12 Piecing diagram for Unit 2
of *Who Stepped on the Duck?***

**5-13 Piecing diagram for sashing in
*Who Stepped on the Duck?***

4. PIECE AND ADD THE SASHING: Sew a small-print spatter-dyed sashing strip between two Unit 2 blocks. Then sew sashing strips to the ends of each block (Fig. 5-13). Repeat with the remaining two blocks.

Sew a Template C piece between two sashing strips. Sew a Template C piece on each end of the sashing strip. Repeat this two more times. Sew one of these pieced sashing strips to each side of a two block unit as in Figure 5-13. Sew the other two block unit to this and then sew the last pieced sashing strip to the edge of that two block unit.

5. PIECE AND ADD THE BORDERS: Attach a border strip to the top and bottom of the quilt. Sew a Template E piece to each end of the other border strips. Add the borders according to the piecing diagram in Figure 5-10.

6. QUILT: Delores Stemple quilted in the ditch of all the seams and ¼" from the edge of all large triangles. She quilted diagonal lines in the blue rectangles in each block and channel-quilted the borders.

84

Flying Dutchman, 44" x 44", by Cynthia Myerberg (Morgantown, West Virginia); machine-pieced, hand-quilted.

FLYING DUTCHMAN

A purchased printed batik-pattern fabric was the starting point for this masculine-looking quilt. Scraps of mottled fabric in light, medium, and dark values were used along with a black crunch-dyed background. The purchased batik-print fabric is the perfect complement for the mottled and crunched fabric.

NAME OF QUILT: *Flying Dutchman*

FINISHED QUILT SIZE: 44" x 44"

SKILL LEVEL: Beginner/Intermediate

FABRIC CHART

Fabric	Amount
Light green mottled dyed	¼ yard
Medium green mottled dyed	¼ yard
Periwinkle mottled dyed	¼ yard
Dark blue mottled dyed	¼ yard
Black commercial batik	1½ yards*
Black crunch-dyed	2 yards

*This includes enough fabric to make 2½"-wide bias binding for the quilt.

Making the Quilt

1. DYE THE FABRIC: To create all of the mottled fabrics (light green, medium green, periwinkle, and dark blue), refer to "Immersion Dyeing: Mottled and Tie-Dye Variation" on page 7. The black crunch-dyed fabric was immersion-dyed after being crunched in a bag according to the technique on page 20. If you crunch the fabric into a tight ball before dyeing, you'll end up with the many light areas that show up on the borders of this quilt.

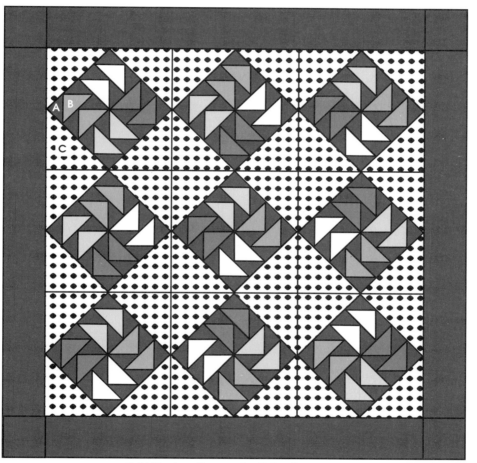

5-14 Piecing diagram for *Flying Dutchman*.

FABRIC KEY

- ☐ Light green mottled dyed
- ☐ Periwinkle mottled dyed
- ☐ Medium green mottled dyed
- ☐ Dark blue mottled dyed
- ☐ Black commercial batik
- ☐ Black crunch-dyed

CUTTING CHART

Template or Strip*	Number to Cut	Fabric to Use
Template A	144	Black crunch-dyed
Template B	18	Light green mottled
	18	Medium green mottled
	18	Periwinkle mottled
	18	Dark blue mottled
Template C	36	Black commercial batik
5" x 35"	4	Black crunch-dyed
5" x 5"	4	Black crunch-dyed

*Templates are located at the end cf the chapter. Remember to add ¼" seam allowance to all templates. Measurements for strips *include* ¼" seam allowance.

2. CUT THE FABRIC: Use the chart (above).

3. PIECE THE BLOCKS: Following the piecing diagram in Figure 5-15, sew a Template A piece to each diagonal side of a Template B piece. Repeat. Sew two of these sections together to make Unit 1. Make nine Unit 1 sections in light green, medium green, periwinkle, and dark blue mottled fabric.

Follow the piecing diagram in Figure 5-16 to piece together one each of a light green, a medium green, a periwinkle, and a dark blue Unit 1 section to make Unit 2. Make nine Unit 2 sections.

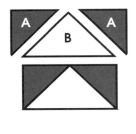

5-15 Piecing diagram for Unit 1 of *Flying Dutchman*.

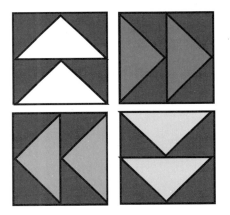

5-16 Piecing diagram for Unit 2 of *Flying Dutchman*.

5-17 Piecing diagram for _Flying Dutchman_ block.

Add four Template C pieces to each Unit 2 section as shown in Figure 5-17 to make nine blocks.

4. SEW THE BLOCKS INTO ROWS: Sew together three of these blocks to create a row, referring to Figure 5-14 as needed. Repeat two more times, and sew together the rows.

5. PIECE AND ADD THE BORDERS: Sew a border strip to the top and botom of the quilt. Sew two corner blocks to each end of the other two border strips. Sew these borders to the quilt top.

6. QUILT: Cynthia quilted in the ditch of all seams and then quilted ¼" from the edge of all of the mottled triangles. She also quilted randomly along the wavy lines of the large batik triangles at 1" intervals. The border is quilted with wavy lines that are 1½" apart.

Shibori-Stripe Frame, 24" x 24", by Joyce Mori (Morgantown, West Virginia); machine-pieced, hand-quilted.

SHIBORI-STRIPE FRAME

The bright blue-on-white shibori stripes are used effectively in this patchwork quilt, forming a frame for the center patchwork motif. Random shibori fabric is easy to do, and the resulting strong stripe motifs can visually set off many designs. Prairie points held down with a large bead form a central pinwheel.

NAME OF QUILT: *Shibori-Stripe Frame*

FINISHED QUILT SIZE: **24" x 24"**

SKILL LEVEL: **Intermediate**

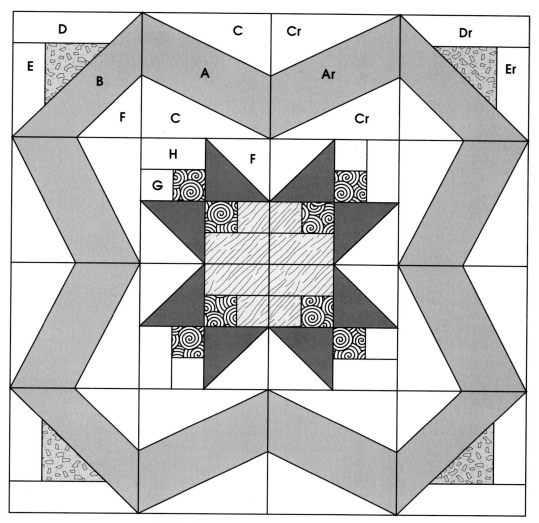

5-18 Piecing diagram for *Shibori-Stripe Frame.*

FABRIC KEY

Blue shibori-stripe

Pale green commercial print

 Multicolor commercial spatter-print

Blue/turquoise commercial print

Dark purple mottled dyed

Medium purple mottled dyed

FABRIC CHART

Fabric	Amount
Blue shibori-stripe	½ yard
Pale green commercial print	1 yard
Multicolor commercial spatter-print	Scrap about 10" square
Blue/turquoise commercial print	Scrap about 14" square
Dark purple mottled dyed	Scrap about 10" square
Medium purple mottled dyed	Scrap about 10" square

CUTTING CHART

Template or Strip*	Number to Cut	Fabric to Use
Template A, Ar	4 each	Blue shibori-stripe
Template B	4	Blue shibori-stripe
Template C, Cr	8 each	Pale green print commercial
Template D, Dr	2 each	Pale green print commercial
Template E, Er	2 each	Pale green print commercial
Template F	4	Commercial spatter-print
	12	Pale green print commercial
	8	Blue/turquoise print
Template G	4	Pale green print commercial
	8	Dark purple mottled dyed
	4	Medium purple mottled dyed
Template H	4	Medium purple mottled dyed
	4	Pale green print commercial

*Templates are located at the end of the chapter. Remember to add ¼" seam allowance to all templates.

Making the Quilt

1. DYE THE FABRIC: To create the shibori-stripe fabric, use one of the shibori-wrap techniques in Chapter 2 and then add blue dye using the direct-dye method. To create the mottled purple fabrics, refer to "Immersion Dyeing: Mottled and Tie-Dye Variation" on page 7.

2. CUT THE FABRIC: Use the chart (above).

3. PIECE THE BLOCKS: Sew two Unit 1 sections and two reversed, following the diagram in Figure 5-19.

Sew four Unit 2 sections and four reversed, following the diagram in Figure 5-20.

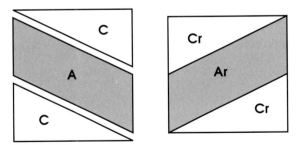

5-20 Piecing diagram for Unit 2 and Unit 2 reversed of _Shibori-Stripe Frame._

Sew four Unit 3 sections, as shown in Figure 5-21.

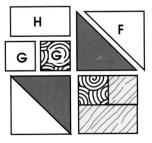

5-21 Piecing diagram for Unit 3 of _Shibori-Stripe Frame._

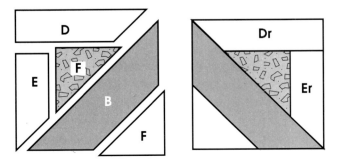

5-19 Piecing diagram for Unit 1 and Unit 1 reversed of _Shibori-Stripe Frame._

4. ADD THE PRAIRIE POINTS: The prairie points form the center pinwheel. To make each prairie point, cut a 3"-square piece of fabric. Fold this in half along the diagonal. Then fold this triangle in half again to produce finished prairie point.

Make four prairie points and pin one to the right side of each Unit 3 block, aligning the long straight edge of the prairie point with the medium purple Template H piece of the block. The prairie points will be flipped into proper position after the blocks are sewn together.

5. SEW THE BLOCKS INTO ROWS: Referring to Figure 5-18 as needed, sew the Unit 1, 2, and 3 blocks into vertical rows. Then sew the rows together. Flip the prairie points into the proper position when the sewing is complete, and sew a large bead to the tip of each point (tacking it to the quilt) to keep it from flipping upward.

6. QUILT: Joyce quilted along some of the lines in the shibori stripe (quilting does not show up well on this fabric) and quilted a square grid on the pale green inside the shibori border.

Hot Flash, 34" x 34", by Cynthia Myerberg (Morgantown, West Virginia); machine-pieced, machine-quilted.

HOT FLASH

Tie dyeing can be lots of fun for all family members. This quilt originated from a large piece of tie-dyed fabric made by Cynthia's son, Jonah Myerberg. He used blue, red, and yellow dye and the direct-dye method to design the fabric. The corners of each block feature blue and red/yellow triangles cut from the tie-dyed fabric. When the blocks are joined together, a pinwheel design appears. Template B pieces were cut from the blue tie-dye areas and from scraps from other projects. Scraps from eight gradations of terra-cotta fabric make up the central portion of each block (to simplify the directions, only four gradations are given in the piecing diagram). Purchased dark blue fabric is used for the border.

NAME OF QUILT: *Hot Flash*

FINISHED QUILT SIZE: 34" x 34"

SKILL LEVEL: Intermediate

FABRIC CHART

Fabric	Amount
Red, yellow, and blue tie-dyed	Approximately 2 yards
Terra-cotta mottled dyed	Scraps, any number of gradations
Dark blue commercial	1½ yards*

*This includes enough fabric to make 2½"-wide bias binding for the quilt.

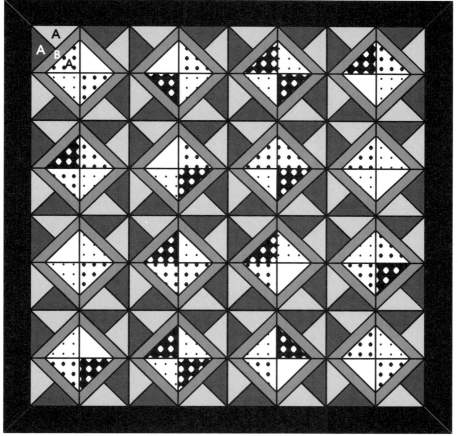

5-22 Piecing diagram for *Hot Flash*.

FABRIC KEY

☐ Red-yellow from tie-dyed

■ Blue from tie-dyed

☐ Terra-cotta gradation #1

☐ Terra-cotta gradation #2

☐ Terra-cotta gradation #3

☐ Terra-cotta gradation #4

☐ Medium blue from tie-dyed and scraps

■ Dark blue commercial

CUTTING CHART

Template or Strip*	Number to Cut	Fabric to Use
Template A	64	Terra-cotta, random gradation
	64	Blue from tie-dyed
	64	Red/yellow tie-dyed
Template B	64	Medium blue tie-dyed or scraps
3½" x 37"	4	Dark blue commercial

*Templates are located at the end of the chapter. Remember to add ¼" seam allowance to all templates. Measurements for strips include ¼" seam allowance.

Making the quilt

1. DYE THE FABRIC: Dye the terra cotta gradations using the "Nine-Step Immersion-Dyed Gradated Sequence" on pages 8–9. Create the tie-dyed fabric using one of the tying methods in Chapter 2 and the direct dyeing technique. Jonah, an experienced tie dyer, dyed a large piece of fabric using red, blue, and yellow dyes and the direct dye method. You could dye several smaller pieces of fabric (22" x 22") and get similar results. The swirl in a ball method is a good one for this project (see page 23). Pour a different color dye in each of the four sections of the tied fabric ball.

2. CUT THE FABRIC: Use the chart (above).

3. PIECE THE BLOCKS: Piece four Unit 1 sections according to Figure 5-23, using a different terra-cotta gradation in each unit. Refer to the overall piecing diagram (Fig. 5-22) as needed.

Sew these four sections together to make a block (Fig. 5-24). Make 16 blocks.

4. SEW THE BLOCKS INTO ROWS: Sew the blocks together, four in a row. Sew the four rows together.

5. ATTACH AND MITER THE BORDERS: Add the dark blue borders and miter the corners (see Step 3 of the *Center Tie-Dye Medallion* quilt on page 68).

6. QUILT: Cynthia machine-quilted in the ditch along all seam lines. She then machine-quilted the tie-dyed triangles along the border with metallic thread, using a free-motion technique.

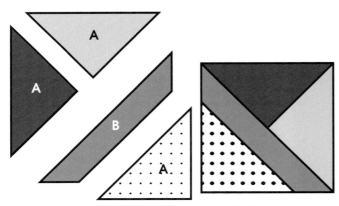

5-23 Piecing diagram for Unit 1 of *Hot Flash*.

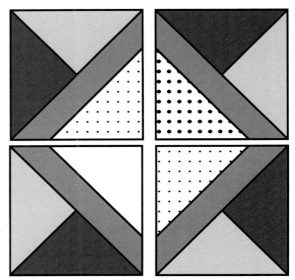

5-24 Piecing diagram for *Hot Flash* block.

Love Knot and Floral Appliqué, 36" x 36", by Joyce Mori (Morgantown, West Virginia);
hand-appliquéd, machine-pieced, and hand-quilted.

LOVE KNOT AND FLORAL APPLIQUÉ

This quilt has a springtime look and uses four shades of green dyed fabric, four types of commercial fabric, a purple mottled dyed fabric, and a peach mottled dyed fabric. The spatter-print commercial fabric in the love knots resembles a hand-painted fabric, as does the purple/turquoise fabric that forms the yo-yo flower heads. Commercial fabrics that imitate hand-dyed or hand-painted fabrics can often blend very nicely with your own hand-dyed or hand-painted fabrics.

NAME OF QUILT: *Love Knot and Floral Appliqué*

FINISHED QUILT SIZE: 36" X 36"

SKILL LEVEL: Beginner

FABRIC CHART

Fabric	Amount
Red commercial spatter-print	Fat quarter (18" x 22")
Dark purple mottled dyed	12" x 12" scrap
Dark green mottled dyed	½ yard
Medium green mottled dyed	¾ yard*
Light green mottled dyed #1	½ yard
Light green mottled dyed #2	½ yard
Dark salmon mottled dyed	12" x 12" scrap
Peach mottled dyed	12" x 12" scrap
Orange and green commercial print	12" x 12" scrap
Purple/turquoise commercial print	12" x 12" scrap

*This includes enough fabric to make 1"-wide straight-edge binding for the quilt.

Making the Quilt

1. DYE THE FABRIC: All of the mottled dyed fabrics (the four values of green, peach, dark salmon, and dark purple) were dyed using the "Immersion Dyeing: Mottled and Tie-Dye Variation" on page 7.

2. CUT THE FABRIC: Use the following chart.

3. PIECE AND APPLIQUÉ THE CENTER BLOCK: Sew the 4 Template L pieces together to form the large center square. Appliqué the large floral motif onto this square, referring to Figure 5-25 as needed. Sew the pieces in the following order: Template I, J, H, and K.

4. PIECE AND APPLIQUÉ THE LOVE KNOTS: Sew a Template C piece to a Template B piece. Repeat this for all C and B pieces to create 24 strips. Sew one of these strips onto each long side of each Template D rectangle piece. Appliqué piece F and then piece E onto piece D in each of these squares. Refer to Figure 5-25 and Templates D, E, and F at the end of the chapter for placement.

CUTTING CHART

Template or Strip*	Number to Cut	Fabric to Use
Template A	12	Dark green mottled
	12	Medium green mottled
	16	Light green mottled #1
Template B	24	Light green mottled #2
Template C	24	Red commercial spatter-print
Template D	12	Light green mottled #2
Template E	12	Dark purple mottled
Template F	12	Red commercial spatter-print
Template G	8	Dark salmon mottled
Template H	4	Peach mottled
Template I	4	Orange and green commercial
Template J	4	Dark salmon mottled
Template K	1	Red commercial spatter-print
Template L	4	Medium green mottled
Template M*	4	Purple/turquoise commercial
Template N	4	Peach mottled

*Templates are located at the end of the chapter. Remember to add ¼" seam allowance to all templates, except M (see Step 7 in quilt instructions).

5. PIECE THE GREEN BACKGROUND BLOCKS:

Referring to Figure 5-25 to make sure you use the correct shades of green, sew each A piece to another A piece so that the two form a square.

6. SEW THE BLOCKS TOGETHER:

Sew the blocks together in horizontal rows. Sew the rows.

7. CREATE AND APPLIQUÉ THE YO-YO FLOWERS:

To make the yo-yo flower heads, cut four Template Ms (do not add seam allowance to the template) from the print you selected. Turn under a ¼" hem around the outside edge and stitch this with a running stitch. Pull the stitch-ing up tight and knot it securely. Finger-press the yo-yo into a circle to get it ready for appliquéing.

Appliqué the yo-yo heads and pieces G and N to the dark green framing triangles, referring to Figure 5-25 and the templates at the end of the chapter as needed.

8. QUILT:

Quilting lines show up very nicely on the solid dyed fabrics, so you may want to use a favorite quilting motif for these areas. Joyce quilted around all of the appliqué motifs and then added two lines of echo quilting around the central flower motif to emphasize it.

5-25 Piecing diagram for *Love Knot and Floral Appliqué*.

FABRIC KEY

- Dark purple mottled dyed
- Dark green mottled dyed
- Medium green mottled dyed
- Light green mottled dyed #1
- Light green mottled dyed #2
- Red commercial print
  (center appliqués use various scraps; see the cutting chart)

September Morning, 40" x 48", by Cynthia Myerberg (Morgantown, West Virginia); machine-pieced, hand-quilted.

SEPTEMBER MORNING

Maple leaves of variegated fall colors dance across a shimmering, jewel-toned background. Three color gradations intersect, giving the quilt luminous movement. Although simple to piece, the use of nine values of each of three colors makes this quilt challenging enough for the experienced quilter.

NAME OF QUILT: *September Morning*

FINISHED QUILT SIZE: **40" x 48"**

SKILL LEVEL: **Advanced**

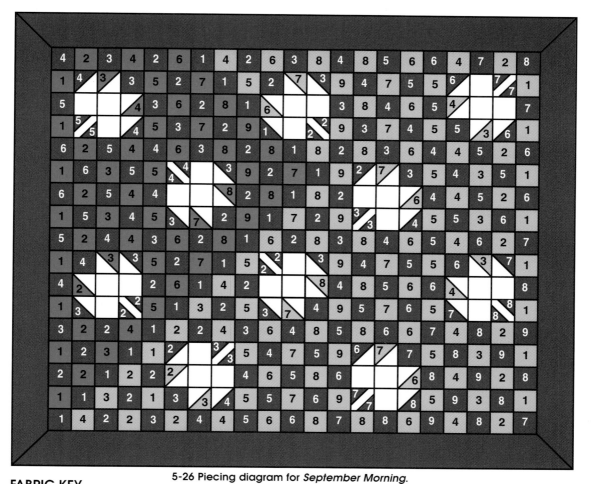

5-26 Piecing diagram for *September Morning*.

FABRIC KEY

■ Purple (numbers = gradation)

▓ Green (numbers = gradation)

▒ Ocher (numbers = gradation)

□ Contrasting fabrics used for leaves

FABRIC CHART

Fabric	Amount
Purple gradation dyed	¼-yard piece for *each* value, 1 through 9
Green gradation dyed	¼-yard piece for *each* value, 1 through 9
Ocher gradation dyed	¼-yard piece for *each* value, 1 through 9
Multicolor dyed	½ yard
Purple mottled dyed	1½ yards

Making the Quilt

1. DYE THE FABRIC: Dye the purple, green, and ocher fabrics using the process outlined under "A Nine-Step Immersion-Dyed Gradated Sequence" on pages 8–9. Dyeing three colors, each in nine gradations, is a good project to do with a friend. Instead of the ¼-yard pieces listed in the Fabric Chart, you could use ½-yard pieces of fabric for each dye bucket, which will give you lots of left-over fabric to share and use in other quilt projects.

The fabric for the maple leaves is direct-dyed using a variety of dye colors. The mottled purple fabric for the border is dyed by using "Immersion

Dyeing: Mottled and Tie-Dye Variation" on page 7.

2. CUT THE FABRIC: In the three charts that follow, the values for each solid color are numbered 1 through 9; #1 is the darkest value and #9 is the lightest value. As you cut out pieces for each color group, stack each value separately and label it with the appropriate value number.

Cutting information for the leaves and borders is given in a separate chart.

Templates are located at the end of the chapter. Remember to add ¼" seam allowances to all templates.

TEMPLATES TO CUT FROM GREEN FABRIC

Value Number	Template A	Template B
#1	8	
#2	6	1
#3	3	2
#4	5	1
#5	6	
#6	5	
#7	4	1
#8	5	1
#9	3	

TEMPLATES TO CUT FROM PURPLE FABRIC

Value Number	Template A	Template B	Template C
#1	16	1	
#2	26	2	6
#3	16	7	4
#4	22	4	2
#5	23		2
#6	15	3	
#7	7	2	4
#8	9	1	2
#9	5		

TEMPLATES TO CUT FROM OCHER FABRIC

Value Number	Template A	Template B
#1	10	
#2	11	1
#3	6	3
#4	12	2
#5	13	
#6	12	3
#7	7	4
#8	14	1
#9	8	

CUTTING CHART FOR LEAVES AND BORDERS

Template or Strip*	Number to Cut	Fabric to Use
Template A	30 (3 for each leaf)	Multicolor dyed
Template B	40 (4 for each leaf)	Multicolor dyed
Template D	10 (1 for each leaf)	Multicolor dyed
3½" x 43"	2	Purple mottled dyed
3½" x 52"	2	Purple mottled dyed

*Templates are located at the end of the chapter. Remember to add ¼" seam allowance to all templates. Measurements for strips *include* ¼" seam allowance.

Row 1 · Row 2 · Row 3 · Row 4 · Row 5 · Row 6 · Row 7 · Row 8 · Row 9 · Row 10 · Row 11 · Row 12 · Row 13 · Row 14 · Row 15 · Row 16 · Row 17 · Row 18 · Row 19 · Row 20 · Row 21

5-27 Piecing diagram for rows of *September Morning*.

3. ARRANGE THE ROWS OF SQUARES: Lay out the cut pieces in 21 vertical rows according to the piecing diagram in Figure 5-27.

4. SEW THE LEAF PIECES: Being careful not to disturb the order of the arranged rows, sew two Template B pieces together as shown in Figure 5-28 to form Unit 1 squares.

5-28 Piecing diagram for Unit 1 of *September Morning*.

Sew Template C and D pieces together as shown in Figure 5-29 to form Unit 2 squares. Place the sewn leaf pieces back into the arranged rows. You will now have 21 rows of squares.

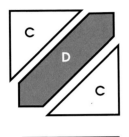

5-29 Piecing diagram for Unit 2 of *September Morning*.

5. SEW THE ROWS: Sew together all the blocks in row 1, from top to bottom. Sew together the blocks in rows 2 through 21. Press seams in opposite directions.

Sew row 1 to row 2, matching seams. Continue in this manner sewing all the rows together. Then press the long seams in one direction.

6. ADD THE BORDERS: Add the borders to the quilt and miter the corners (see Step 3 of the *Center Tie-Dye Medallion* quilt on page 68).

7. QUILT: Cynthia quilted in the ditch along the seam lines in this quilt and added a quilted wave pattern in the border.

The Uglies, 43" x 43", by Joyce Mori (Morgantown, West Virginia); machine-pieced, hand-quilted.

THE UGLIES

This quilt's name has no relationship to its overall appearance. Rather the name refers to the pieces of fabric that were sewn together to complete the quilt. All the fabrics used in this quilt were dyeing rejects: the colors had turned to mud brown, the dye color mixtures were not what was planned, or the direct-dye tie-dye design was not attractive. This wall quilt design is the perfect answer to any "uglies" you create. Once the fabrics are cut up and stripped together, their ugliness disappears!

If you desire, you can also use some commercial fabrics in this quilt in place of the dyed fabrics. It's a good way to get rid of fabrics you no longer find beautiful.

NAME OF QUILT: *The Uglies*

FINISHED SIZE OF QUILT: 43" x 43"

SKILL LEVEL: Intermediate

FABRIC CHART

Fabric	Amount*
Light blue/green commercial	½ yard
Dark purple commercial	Fat quarter (18" x 22")
Medium/light values of dyed "uglies"	1 yards
Dark values of dyed "uglies"	1¼ yards
Dark-value dyed "ugly"	16" x 50"**

*All amounts are approximate and may vary depending on the amount of strip-piecing you do (see Step 2 in quilt instructions).

**This includes enough fabric to make 1"-wide straight edge binding for the quilt.

Making the Quilt

1. CHOOSE THE FABRIC: Sort through your dyed and commercial fabrics to come up with fabrics of light, medium, and dark values. Don't be afraid to combine colors that you wouldn't usually put together. *Value* refers to the lightness or darkness of a color, not the color itself. If you don't have enough fabrics on hand, create some new dyed and painted fabrics using the techniques described in Chapters 1 through 3.

2. STRIP-PIECE SCRAPS FOR CUTTING: Templates A, D, and E are cut from strip-pieced fabric (see Fig. 5-30). You will cut narrow strips of fabric and sew like-valued strips together to create pieces from which the templates can be cut.

You can cut all your strips the same width or vary them. The strips in the photographed quilt range from ¾" to 1½" in width, meaning that they were 1¼" to 2" wide before they were sewn together.

Do not make your strip-pieced scraps too long or the seam lines will cause the fabric to bow. Create pieces that are just bigger than the templates you want to cut. Remember you need 20 A pieces, 16 D pieces, and 4 E pieces (see Cutting Chart in Step 3), and you may want to cut several from the same piece.

You will also need to decide the direction of your strips. Notice the direction of the stripped pieces in Figure 5-30. Feel free to deviate from the directions shown. You could make the strips run lengthwise or, in the A pieces, have them run parallel to the diagonal side of the triangle.

Remember, you can always substitute a whole piece of "ugly" fabric where stripped pieces are shown.

3. CUT THE FABRIC: Use the following chart.

CUTTING CHART		
Template or Strip*	Number to Cut	Fabric to Use
Template A	48	Dark-value "uglies" (20 strip-pieced)
Template B, Br	16 each	Light blue/green commercial
Template C	16	Dark purple commercial
Template D	16	Light-value "uglies" (all strip-pieced)
Template E	4	Light-value "uglies" (all strip-pieced)
2" x 45"**	4	Dark-value "ugly"

*Templates are located at the end of the chapter. Remember to add ¼" seam allowance to all templates. Measurements for strips *include* ¼" seam allowance.

**Cut these border strips *after* you have assembled the quilt top. See Step 5 of the quilt instructions.

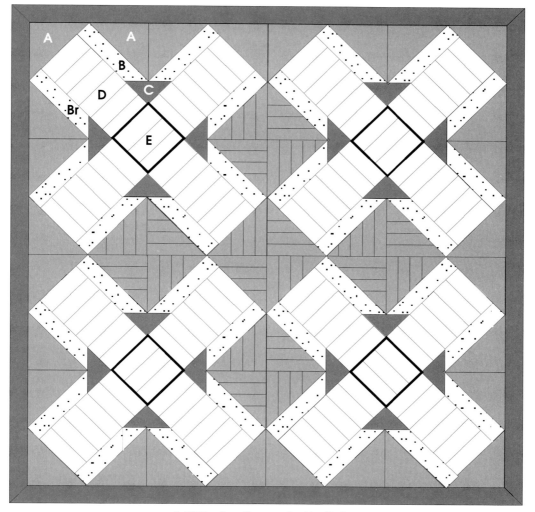

5-30 Piecing diagram for *The Uglies.*

FABRIC KEY

Dark purple commercial

Medium/light dyed "uglies"

Dark dyed "uglies"

Light blue/green commercial

4. PIECE THE BLOCKS: To create Unit 1, sew one A piece to a B piece and another A piece to a Br piece as shown in Figure 5-31. Sew these two together, and then sew a C piece at the tip of the squared-off triangle. Refer to Figure 5-30 to check the direction of your strip-pieced sections.

Sew a D piece between two Unit 1 sections. Sew an A piece to the outside edge of the D piece to create Unit 2 (see Fig. 5-31). Repeat this once more.

Sew an E piece between two D pieces. Sew this strip between two Unit 2 pieces.

Attach an A triangle to each open edge of the D strip so that a square is formed (see Fig. 5-31). You have completed one block. Sew three more blocks like this one, and sew them together according to Figure 5-30.

5. ADD AND MITER THE BORDERS: For mitering instructions, refer to Step 3 of the *Center Tie-Dye Medallion* quilt on page 68. Be sure to check your final measurements before cutting the border fabric pieces. The measurement in the Cutting Chart allows extra length beyond the miter, but your quilt top may measure slightly different from ours. Attach and miter the borders according to the directions given.

6. QUILT: Joyce quilted in the ditch of this quilt and added extra lengthwise quilting lines in many of the strips.

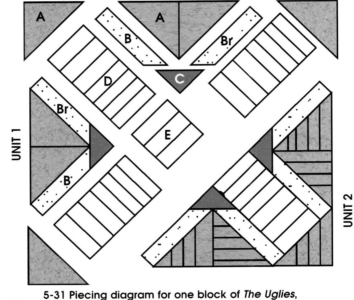

5-31 Piecing diagram for one block of *The Uglies*, including Units 1 and 2.

JANE'S COLORS TEMPLATES AND PLACEMENT GUIDES

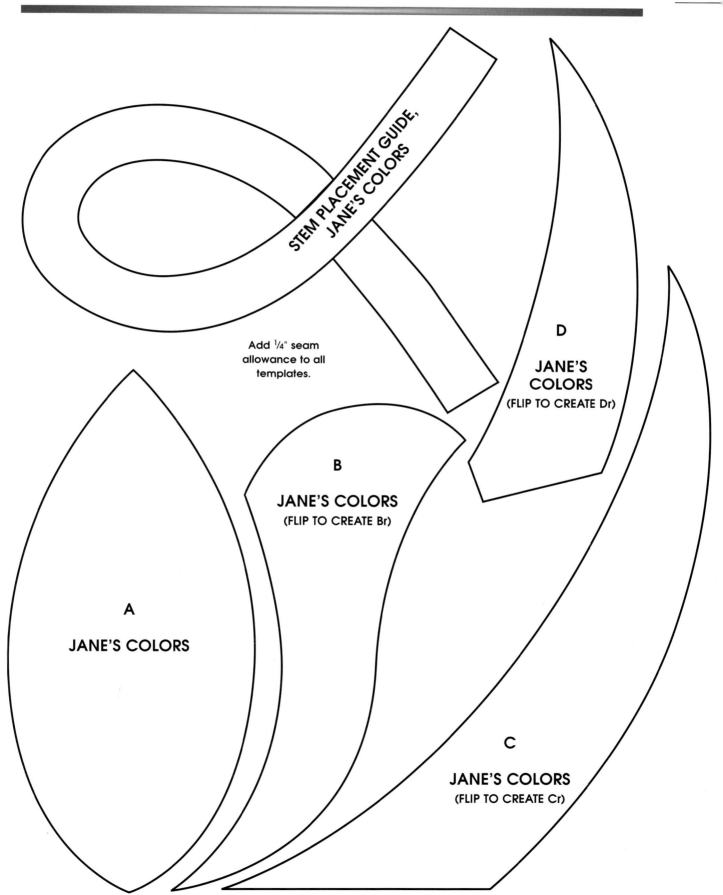

STEM PLACEMENT GUIDE,
JANE'S COLORS

Add ¼" seam
allowance to all
templates.

D

JANE'S
COLORS
(FLIP TO CREATE Dr)

B

JANE'S COLORS
(FLIP TO CREATE Br)

A

JANE'S COLORS

C

JANE'S COLORS
(FLIP TO CREATE Cr)

STEM PLACEMENT GUIDE, JANE'S COLORS

SPRING IS HERE TEMPLATES AND PLACEMENT GUIDE

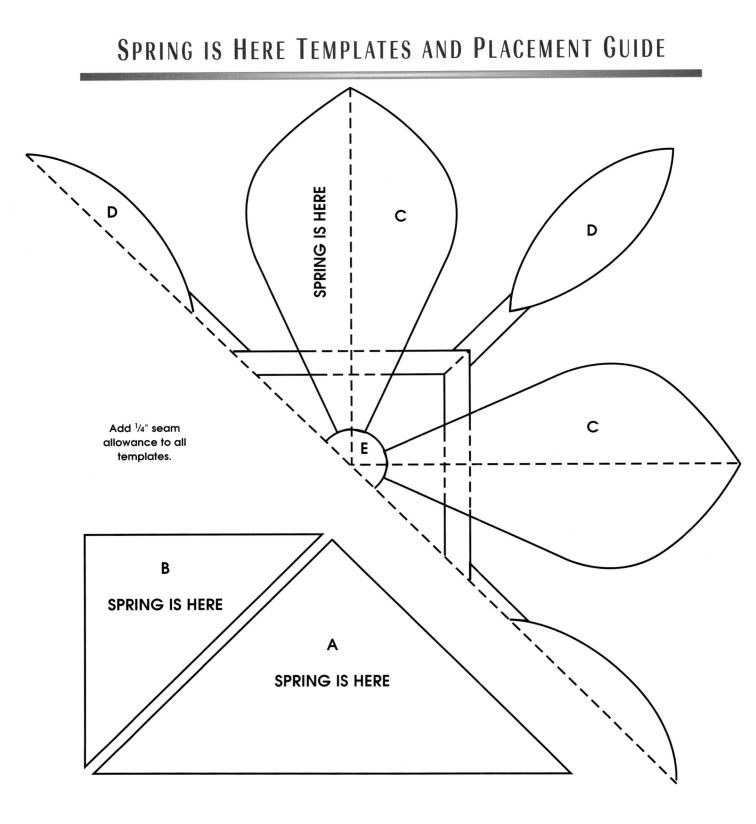

SPRING IS HERE

C

D

Add ¼" seam allowance to all templates.

E

C

D

B

SPRING IS HERE

A

SPRING IS HERE

AMISH SQUARE IN A SQUARE TEMPLATES

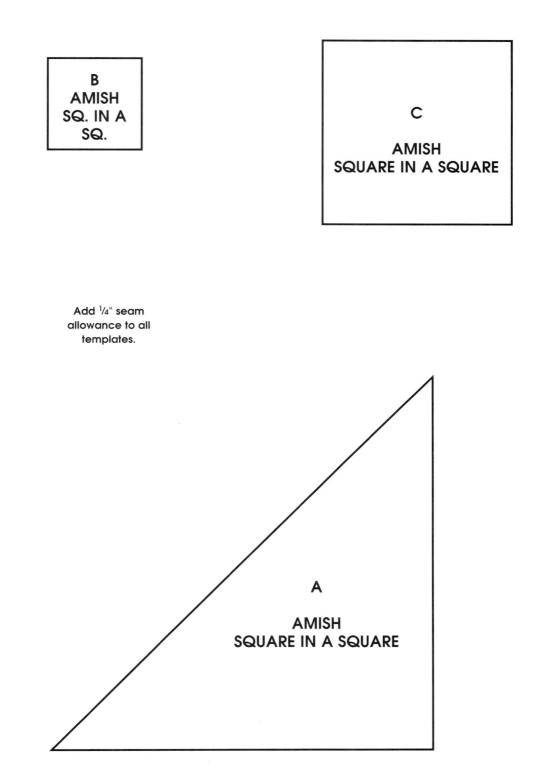

B AMISH SQ. IN A SQ.

C AMISH SQUARE IN A SQUARE

Add ¼" seam allowance to all templates.

A AMISH SQUARE IN A SQUARE

WHO STEPPED ON THE DUCK? TEMPLATES

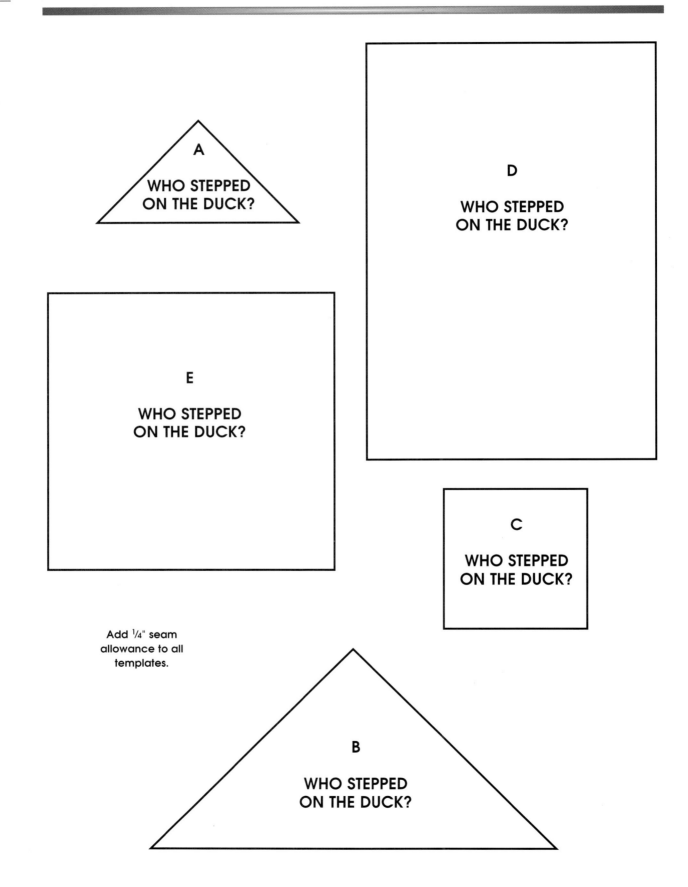

A

WHO STEPPED
ON THE DUCK?

D

WHO STEPPED
ON THE DUCK?

E

WHO STEPPED
ON THE DUCK?

C

WHO STEPPED
ON THE DUCK?

Add ¼" seam
allowance to all
templates.

B

WHO STEPPED
ON THE DUCK?

FLYING DUTCHMAN TEMPLATES

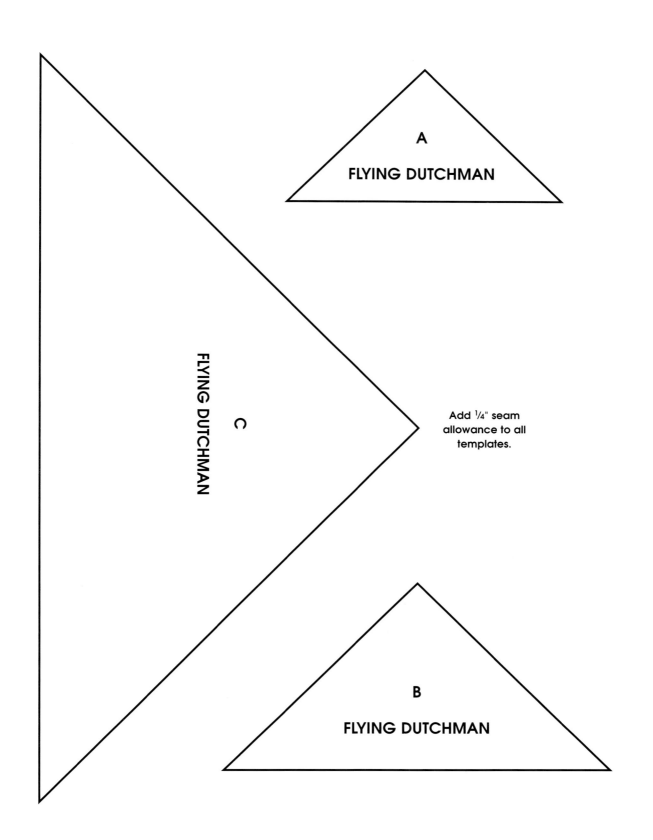

A
FLYING DUTCHMAN

FLYING DUTCHMAN
C

Add ¼" seam
allowance to all
templates.

B
FLYING DUTCHMAN

SHIBORI-STRIPE FRAME TEMPLATES

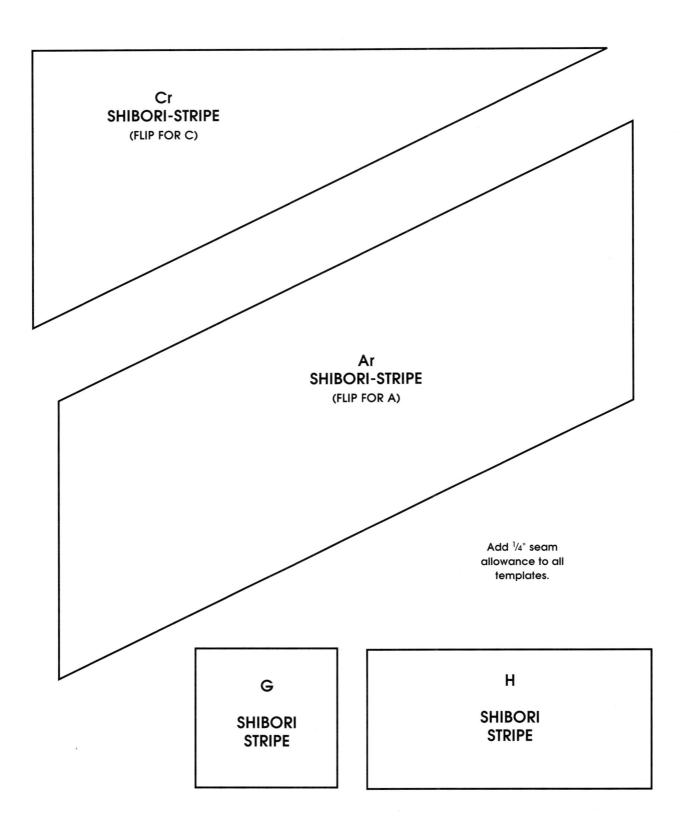

Cr
SHIBORI-STRIPE
(FLIP FOR C)

Ar
SHIBORI-STRIPE
(FLIP FOR A)

Add ¼" seam
allowance to all
templates.

G

**SHIBORI
STRIPE**

H

**SHIBORI
STRIPE**

Add ¼" seam allowance to all templates.

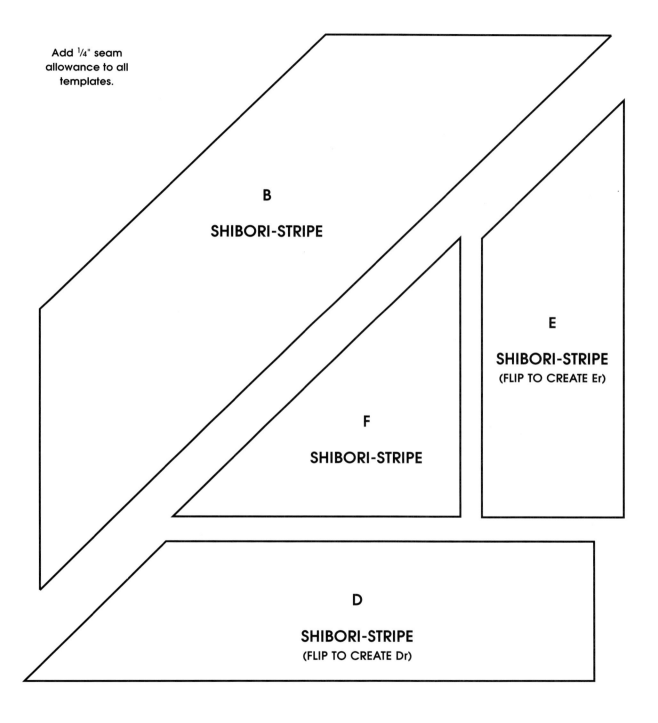

B

SHIBORI-STRIPE

E

SHIBORI-STRIPE
(FLIP TO CREATE Er)

F

SHIBORI-STRIPE

D

SHIBORI-STRIPE
(FLIP TO CREATE Dr)

Hot Flash Templates

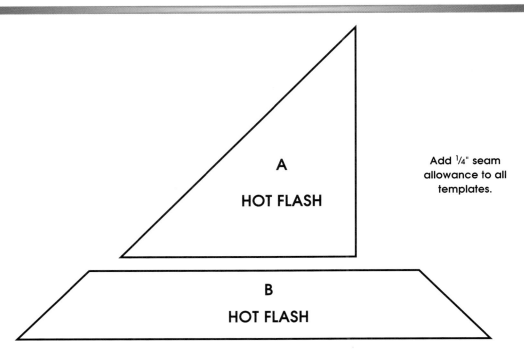

A

HOT FLASH

Add ¼" seam allowance to all templates.

B

HOT FLASH

Love Knot and Floral Appliqué Templates

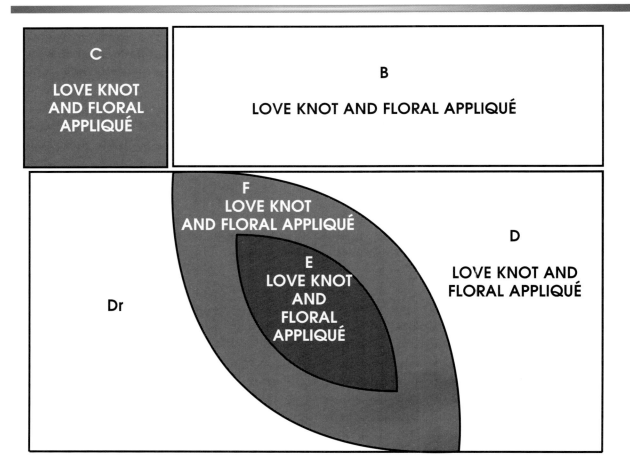

C

LOVE KNOT AND FLORAL APPLIQUÉ

B

LOVE KNOT AND FLORAL APPLIQUÉ

F
LOVE KNOT AND FLORAL APPLIQUÉ

D

LOVE KNOT AND FLORAL APPLIQUÉ

E
LOVE KNOT AND FLORAL APPLIQUÉ

Dr

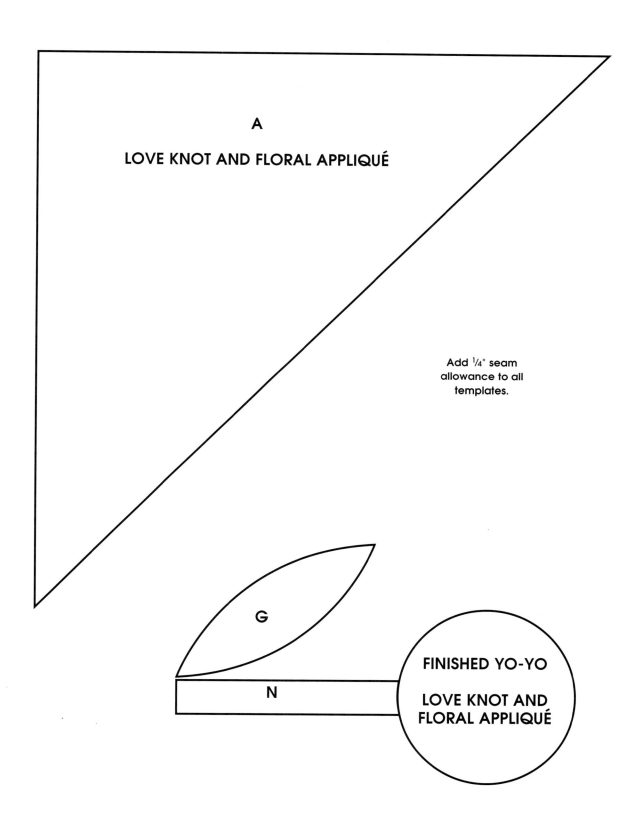

A

LOVE KNOT AND FLORAL APPLIQUÉ

Add ¼" seam
allowance to all
templates.

G

N

FINISHED YO-YO

LOVE KNOT AND
FLORAL APPLIQUÉ

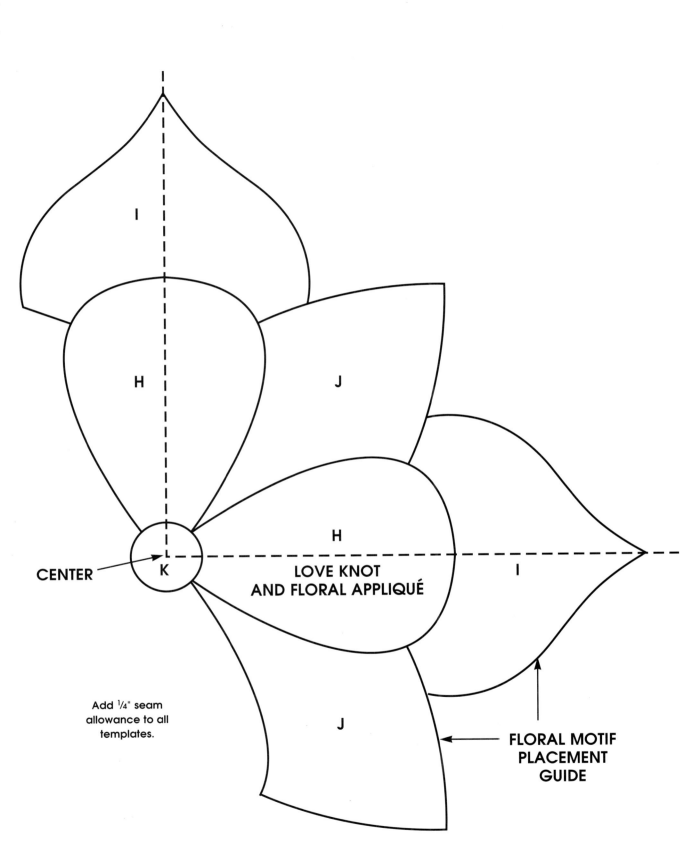

I

H

J

CENTER

K

LOVE KNOT
AND FLORAL APPLIQUÉ

H

I

Add ¼" seam
allowance to all
templates.

J

FLORAL MOTIF
PLACEMENT
GUIDE

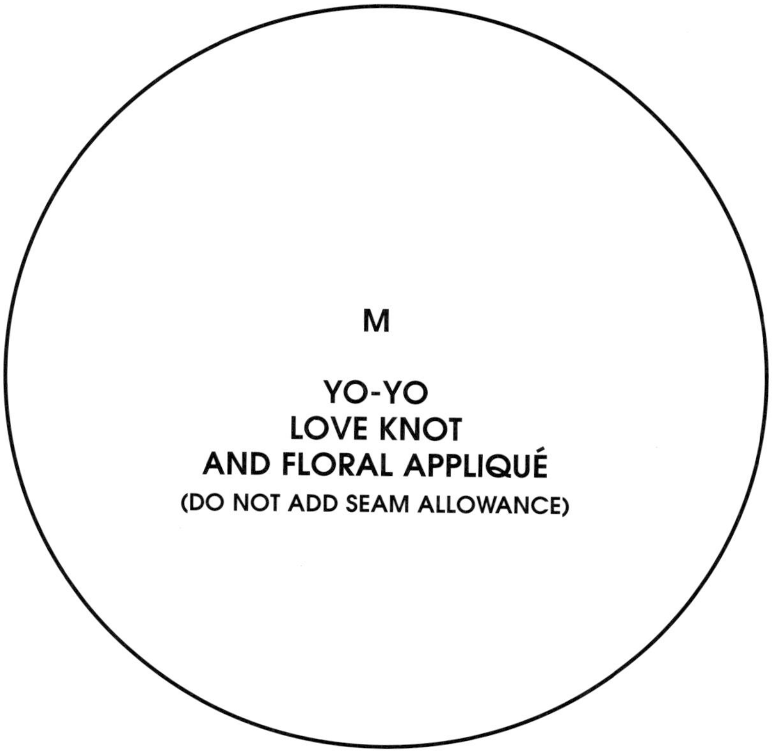

M

YO-YO
LOVE KNOT
AND FLORAL APPLIQUÉ
(DO NOT ADD SEAM ALLOWANCE)

Add ¼" seam
allowance to all
templates.

L

LOVE KNOT
AND FLORAL APPLIQUÉ

SEPTEMBER MORNING TEMPLATES

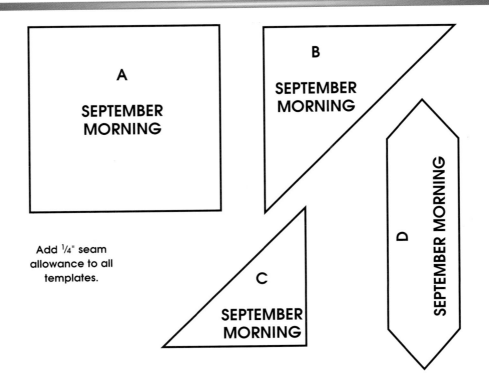

A

SEPTEMBER MORNING

B

SEPTEMBER MORNING

C

SEPTEMBER MORNING

D

SEPTEMBER MORNING

Add ¼" seam allowance to all templates.

THE UGLIES TEMPLATES

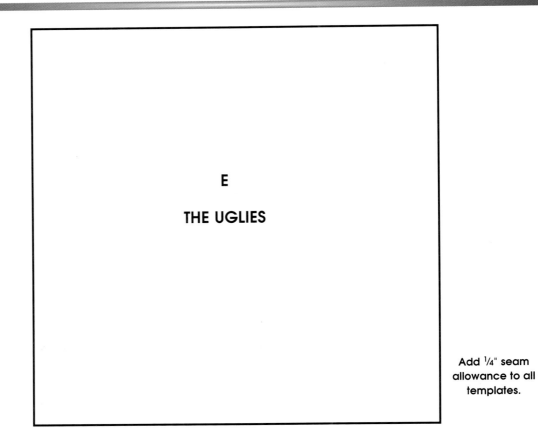

E

THE UGLIES

Add ¼" seam allowance to all templates.

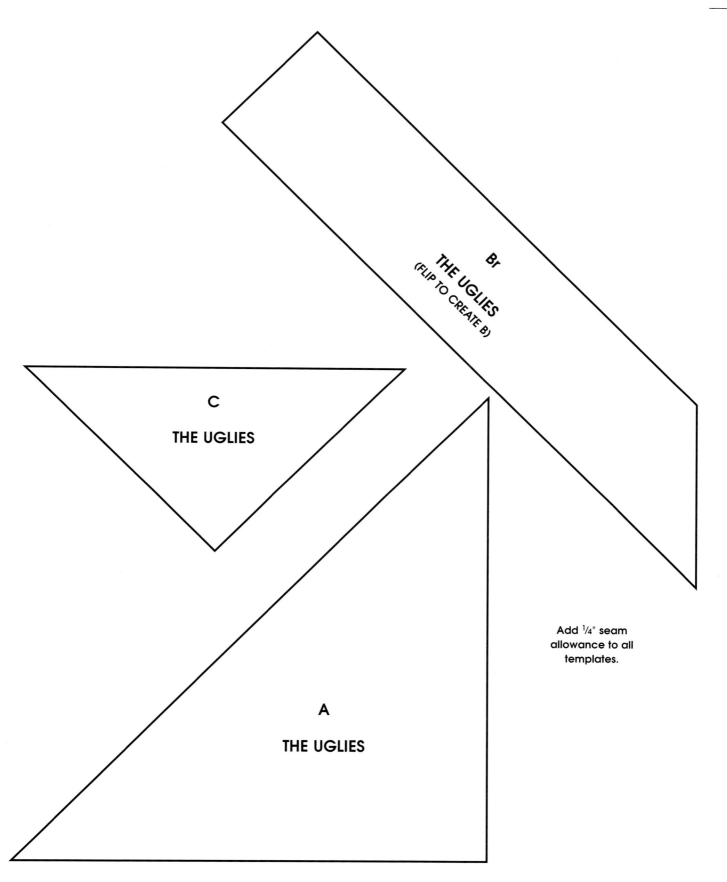

Br
THE UGLIES
(FLIP TO CREATE B)

C
THE UGLIES

Add ¼" seam allowance to all templates.

A
THE UGLIES

120

D

THE UGLIES

Add ¼" seam
allowance to all
templates.

MORE USES FOR DYED AND PAINTED FABRIC

Wearable Art and Designer Clothing

It is easy to have one-of-a-kind designer clothing (or "wearable art") when you make your garments from your own dyed or painted fabric. Scraps can be pieced or strip-pieced and used to construct, accent, or embellish any garment. You can dye or paint larger amounts of fabric to make an entire garment. Try using dyed or painted fabrics with your favorite purchased pattern to make your own designer creation.

DAYTIME AND EVENING WEAR

The two ensembles shown on the following page are made of 100% viscous rayon that was dyed by the crunch-in-a-bag method using the process outlined under "Immersion Dyeing: Mottled and Tie-Dye Variation" on page 7. Cynthia Myerberg is wearing a blue/green over-

Hand-dyed and hand-painted fabrics create truly original wearable art.

sized shirt over a flared skirt. An appliquéd and quilted vest adds an artistic accent. Her daughter, Nalini Pillai, is wearing a two-piece pantsuit. A 100% silk scarf, dyed to match, is used for a belt. Both ensembles were made by Cynthia Myerberg.

To find 100% viscous rayon that is suitable for dyeing, contact some of the supply sources listed in Appendix A. Viscous rayon is usually 54" wide. Some shrinkage occurs when this fabric is prescoured and dried, so order somewhat more fabric than you need. For best results, dye lengths of 1½ yards or less.

Dyeing Process

Dye the fabric based on the "Immersion Dye: Mottled and Tie-Dye Variation" on page 7 and the crunch-in-a-bag tie-dye method on page 20, with the following modifications.

1. After the fabric has been prescoured and machine-dried, note the amount that you will need for each component of the outfit and cut the fabric into appropriate lengths. For the blue/green ensemble, a 1½-yard length of 54" rayon was dyed for the shirt and another 1½-yard length was dyed for the skirt. The leftover fabric was used to line and bind the edges of the vest.

2. Crunch each piece of rayon into a ball and place it on a large piece of nylon net or tulle. Bring the corners and edges of the net or tulle together around the fabric bundle and tie it with string. (*Note:* Do not make the bundle too compact, or the dye will not penetrate to the center of the bundle.)

3. Be sure to wet each fabric bundle thoroughly in plain water and squeeze out excess moisture before you put the fabric into the dye bath.

4. Dye both 1½-yard bundles of fabric in the same dye bath, which requires the following:

- 2 gallons room-temperature water

- 1 cup noniodized salt

- 3 tablespoons green dye and 3 tablespoons blue dye mixed with water to make 2 cups of dye solution

- 4 tablespoons of dye activator dissolved in two cups of hot water (for use in Step 8 of the immersion dyeing process).

5. When you stir the dye bath, gently squeeze the bundles (with your rubber-gloved hands) to ensure that dye reaches their centers.

6. Be sure to afterwash the dyed fabric twice because it is a large amount of fabric.

The dyed rayon is now soft and easy to sew. You can machine-wash and machine-dry the finished garment.

The vest is made from direct-dyed 100% silk noil that was machine-appliquéd with scraps of silk noil and rayon that were cut freehand in curvilinear forms. Metallic thread was used to machine-quilt the vest in the free-motion style.

The fabric for the fuchsia outfit was made using the same amount of fabric and the same dye bath measurements as given for the blue/green outfit, except that 3 tablespoons of fuchsia dye powder was substituted for the blue and green dyes.

WATERCOLOR SUNFLOWER VEST

The vest (shown upper-right on the next page) is painted rather than dyed and is very easy to make. The lining is made from purchased fabric.

Making the Vest

1. Prewash your fabric.

2. Cut out the vest pieces.

3. Draw your sunflowers at the bottom of each vest piece, on the right side, using your favorite washout pen/pencil. Outline each flower and leaf with a black permanent pen (we find Pigma brand works best). Let this dry.

4. Soak your vest pieces in water so that they are thoroughly wet. Let the excess water drip off. Paint the sunflowers and leaves with a very

124

watery paint. Use an eyedropper to run a line of paint down the center of each petal. The paint will wick to the outside edges and beyond the lines of the petal. To slow down the wicking

action, use a blow dryer to quickly dry the fabric.

5. Paint the stems and leaves with the tip of a 1" foam brush with green paint that has a thicker

Hand-painted sunflower vest; two strip-pieced vests made from dyed fabrics;
a woman's tie made from shibori-stripe fabric; a crunch-dyed T-shirt.

consistency than the paint used in Step 4. This method produces less of a wicking action.

6. Let the vest dry. Set the paint according to manufacturer's directions.

7. Now, soak only the top of each vest section in water to prepare the area for painting. Apply a very thin paint in a couple rows across the top of the vest sections and brush it in with a foam brush. Hang the pieces on a line so the paint runs down into the flower area. Once the paint has run the way you want, allow the vest pieces to dry flat on your worktable. Place paper towels under each painted section to soak up excess paint.

8. Set the paint according to manufacturer's directions and then sew your vest pieces together.

DYED VESTS

These two vests are perfect projects for you to sew using fabric strips from your dyeing and/or painted experiments. The vests showcase various dyed fabrics and are the perfect personal reward for all of your work.

Sewing strips to a foundation fabric will result in a garment that has more body. Refer to the following directions.

Making a Vest on Foundation Fabric

1. Select an easy-to-sew vest pattern, preferably one without darts, and then select a foundation fabric. (Because the foundation fabric is not seen, you can use failed dyeing experiments or other scrap fabric.) Cut out the vest pattern pieces from your foundation fabric, allowing ½" additional fabric around the outside edges of the pattern pieces.

2. Cut out strips of your dyed and/or painted fabrics. To add extra interest to the vest, vary the size of the strips. The widths you choose may depend on the design you have dyed on the fabric. Try to cut strips that show off terrific color combinations and exciting designs.

3. Always start at an edge of the pattern piece and work across or down. For example, you could start at the shoulder seam, laying your first strip parallel to that seam, and work down.

4. Lay the first strip, right side up, on the foundation fabric so that it is flush with the shoulder seam. Pin it in place. Place the second strip right side down on top of the first strip. Sew the two strips to the foundation fabric ¼" from the bottom edge of the strips.

5. Flip the second strip over so it is right side up. Pin it flat to the foundation fabric and place a third strip, right side down, on top of it. Sew the second and third strips to the foundation fabric at their bottom-most edge with a ¼" seam. Proceed down the garment in this manner until you have covered the pattern piece.

6. If you want to embellish your strips, consider sewing prairie points into one of the seams, as was done on the multicolor vest. Refer to Step 4 of the *Shibori-Stripe Frame* quilt on page 91.

7. Once your strips are sewn onto the foundation piece, cut the piece to the exact size of the pattern.

8. Sew the pieces of the vest together and embellish as desired. The blue vest has a ½" bias bar strip appliquéd onto the edge of the false collar. The multicolor vest has a bias edging sewn around all outside edges so the vest is reversible.

WOMAN'S TIE

An attractive reddish-purple shibori fabric was used for this tie (shown bottom-right in photo on facing page), which could highlight a favorite blouse or dress. An adjustable ribbon makes it fit different collar sizes.

Gifts, accessories, and decorator items can be

Decorator and Accessory Items

made from dyed and painted fabric. We have shown only a small sample of these items, but you will find many more innovative uses for your original fabric.

feature stamped fabric. The ends of thread spools, round erasers, and other "found" items were used as the stamps.

PLACEMAT

A tie-dyed and a solid-colored dyed fabric were combined with a commercial fabric to make the placemats. The edges of the placemats

TRAVEL PILLOWS

These travel pillows were covered with bright tie-dyed fabrics. You will never leave these in a motel!

Decorator and accessory items.

A collection of dyed scarves.

BOOK COVER AND BOOKMARK

Start a daily journal and make the book special by covering it with one of your original tie-dyed fabrics. Add a bookmark for a special touch.

BELT

Use your own dyed or painted fabric and your favorite belt pattern to create a one-of-a-kind belt. Multicolored direct-dyed 100% silk noil was used to make this unusual belt. Pleats were formed and pressed in different directions to create an undulating effect.

SCRUNCHIE

Green-and-white shibori-patterned 100% viscous rayon was used to make this unusual scrunchie. This is a great gift item for any young woman with long hair.

PILLOW WITH RUFFLE

A challenge block not pictured elsewhere in this book, *Three Dimensional Dahlia* by Kay Beamer of Morgantown, West Virginia, was used to make this stunning decorator pillow. Fabric for the large petals was made by the swirl-in-a-ball tie-dye method and immersion-dyed in a turquoise dye bath. The same fabric was dyed again in a violet dye bath using the crunch-in-a-bag method. The small red-violet petals were made from mottled fabric. The light turquoise background and the medium turquoise center circle were also mottled. The ruffle is a coordinating commercial print.

SCARVES

White 100% silk or 100% cotton scarf blanks can be purchased from fabric supply sources (listed in Appendix A) and then dyed using any of the methods described in this book. The red-orange scarf was dyed by the crunch-in-a-bag method. The turquoise scarf was folded in half and shibori-wrapped.

The photo on page 127 features a variety of dyed scarves ranging from subtle, understated colors to bold and vibrant hues. Choose your colors and patterns to match your favorite outfits. These scarves also make great impromptu gift items.

APPENDIX A

MAIL-ORDER SOURCES FOR SUPPLIES

ALJO MFG. CO.
81 Franklin St.
New York, NY 10013
(212) 966-4046 or (212) 226-2878
Dye, chemicals

COLORADO WHOLESALE DYE CORP.
2139 S. Sheridon Blvd.
Denver, CO 80227
1-800-697-1566
Dye, chemicals

DHARMA TRADING CO.
P.O. Box 150916
San Rafael, CA 94915
(415) 456-7657
1-800-542-5227
Dye, fabric, fabric paint, chemicals

DICK BLICK ART MATERIALS
P.O. Box 1267
Galesburg, IL 61402-1267
1-800-447-8192
Fabric paint, art supplies, dye, chemicals

EARTH GUILD
33 Haywood St. Dept FA
Asheville, NC 28801
1-800-327-8448
Dye, chemicals, fabric paint

FABDEC
3553 Old Post Road
San Angelo, TX 76904
(915) 653-6170 (day)
(915) 942-0571 (evening)
Dyes, chemicals, fabric

GLAD CREATIONS
3400 Bloomington Avenue South
Minneapolis, MN 55407
(612) 724-1079
Ask for #7878 muslin.
Fabrics

LUNN FABRICS, INC.
357 North Santa Fe Drive
Denver, CO 80223
(303) 623-2710
FAX (303) 623-7202
Orders: 1-800-934-6211
Fabrics

PRO CHEMICAL & DYE, INC.
P.O. Box 14
Somerset, MA 02726
1-800-228-9393
(508) 676-3838
FAX (508) 676-3980
Dye, fabric, fabric paint, chemicals

RUPERT, GIBBON & SPIDER, INC.
P.O. Box 425
Healdsburg, CA 95448
1-800-442-0455
Fax (707) 433-4906
Dye, chemicals, paints, fabric

SAY ARTS AND CRAFTS
P.O. Box 51701
New Berlin, WI 53151
1-800-558-6696
1-800-242-9411, WI
Fabric paints, dye, chemicals, fabric

TESTFABRICS, INC.
P.O. Box 420
Middlesex, NJ 08846
(908) 469-6446
Fabrics

APPENDIX B

FABRIC PAINT BRANDS

The following are some of the brands of paint you can use. The list is not complete, but it illustrates the range of paints you can find in stores or mail-order catalogs.

BADGER AIR-TEX

CRAYOLA CRAFT

CREATEX AIRBRUSH COLORS

DEKA PERMANENT FABRIC PAINTS

DEKA PERMANENT FABRIC PAINTS in metallic colors

DEKA SILK

DEKA TEXTILE SCREENING INK

DELTA CREAMCOAT

JAQUARD TEXTILE COLORS

LUMIERE FABRIC PAINT

PEINTEX

POLYMARK DIMENSIONAL FABRIC AND CRAFT PAINT

PROFAB TEXTILE INKS

PRO TEXTILE AIR BRUSH COLORS

SCRIBBLES DIMENSIONAL FABRIC AND CRAFT PAINT

SETACOLOR

SLICK FABRIC PAINT

SPEEDBALL TEXTILE SCREEN PRINTING INK

STARBRIGHT FABRIC PAINT

TEXTICOLOR IRIDESCENT FABRIC PAINT

TULIP FABRIC PAINTS: Spatter Paints, Puffy Paints, Glitter Paints, Slick Paints

VERSATEX AIRBRUSH PRINTING INK

VERSATEX PRINTING PAINT

APPENDIX C

DYE RECIPES

The following dye recipes are for immersion dyeing a ½-yard length of fabric in a 1-gallon dye bath. A dark-to-medium value of the color will be produced. If you like the color and wish to do eight or nine gradations of that color, double the amount of dye in the recipe.

RED
1½ teaspoons Fuchsia MX-8B

TERRA-COTTA
3 tablespoons Yellow MX-4G
2 teaspoons Fuchsia MX-8B
¼ teaspoon Turquoise MX-G

RED/TERRA-COTTA
2 tablespoons Yellow MX-4G
2 teaspoons Fuchsia MX-8B
1/16 teaspoon Turquoise MX-G

TERRA-COTTA PEACH
1 tablespoon PRO Wisteria 820
1 tablespoon PRO Peach 210

RED-ORANGE
2 tablespoons Yellow MX-4G
2 teaspoons Fuchsia MX-8B

RED-VIOLET
2 teaspoons Basic Blue MX-R
2 teaspoons Fuchsia MX-8B

YELLOW
3 tablespoons Yellow MX-4G

OCHER
2 tablespoons Yellow MX-4G
½ teaspoon Brown MX5-BR

BRONZE
1 tablespoon Brown MX-GRN
½ teaspoon Turquoise MX-G

BROWN MAHOGANY
2 teaspoons PRO 5213 Rust Brown
½ teaspoon PRO 6228 Pewter
½ teaspoon PRO 5209 Khaki

BLUE
1½ teaspoons Blue MX-R

SOFT NAVY
2 tablespoons Navy MX-2RDA
¾ teaspoon Turquoise MX-G

BLUE-GREEN
1½ tablespoons Basic Blue MX-R
2 teaspoons Green MX-CBA

TEAL
1 tablespoon Basic Blue MX-R
1 tablespoon Green MX-CBA

TEAL-GREEN
3 teaspoons PRO Green 700N
½ teaspoon Navy MX-2 RDA
¾ teaspoon Turquoise MX-G

BLUE-VIOLET
1 tablespoon Basic Blue MX-R
½ teaspoon Fuchsia MX-8B

PURPLE
1 tablespoon Basic Blue MX-R
2 teaspoons Fuchsia MX-8B

PERIWINKLE
A light value of Blue-Violet

MAUVE
1 tablespoon PRO 331 Cherry Blush
1 teaspoon Turquoise MX-G

GREEN
1½ tablespoons Green MX-CBA

LIME-GREEN
2 tablespoons Yellow MX-4G
2 teaspoons Basic Blue MX-R

LIGHT OLIVE
1 tablespoon Yellow MX-3RA
1½ teaspoons PRO 444 Baby Blue

BLACK
3 tablespoons Black MX-CWNA

Appendix D

QUILTING DIAGRAMS FOR COLORING

Center Tie-Dye Medallion

JANE'S COLORS

SPRING IS HERE

AMISH SQUARE IN A SQUARE

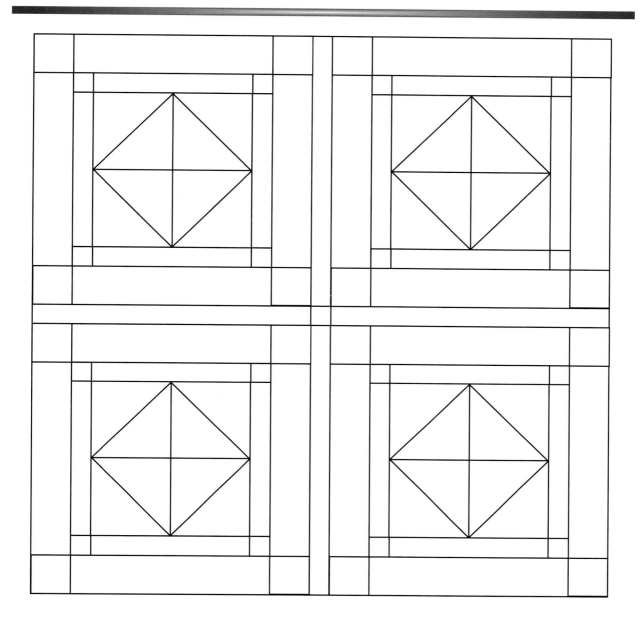

WHO STEPPED ON THE DUCK?

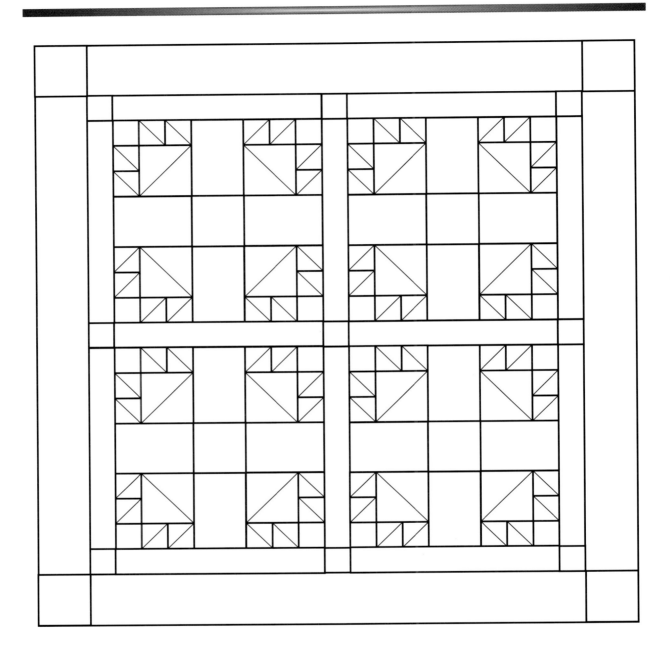

FLYING DUTCHMAN

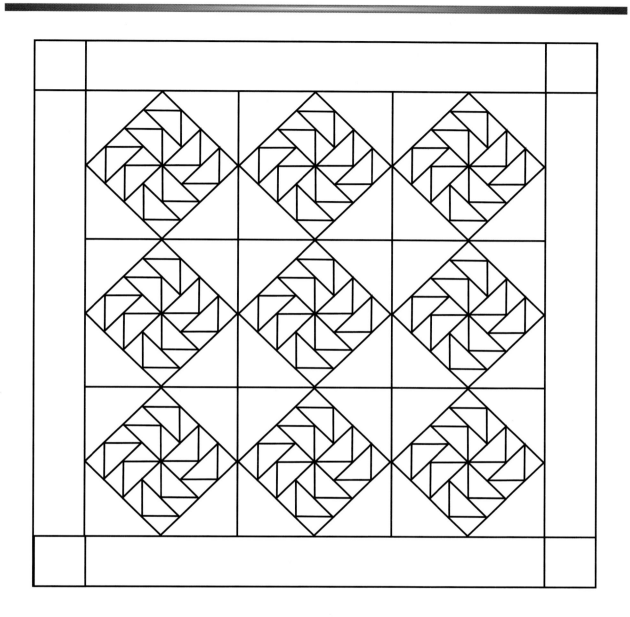

SHIBORI-STRIPE FRAME

HOT FLASH

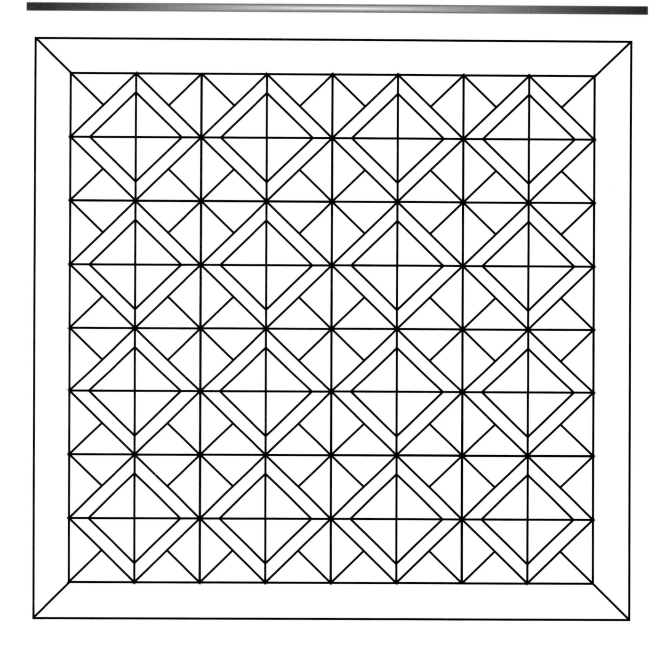

LOVE KNOT AND FLORAL APPLIQUÉ

SEPTEMBER MORNING

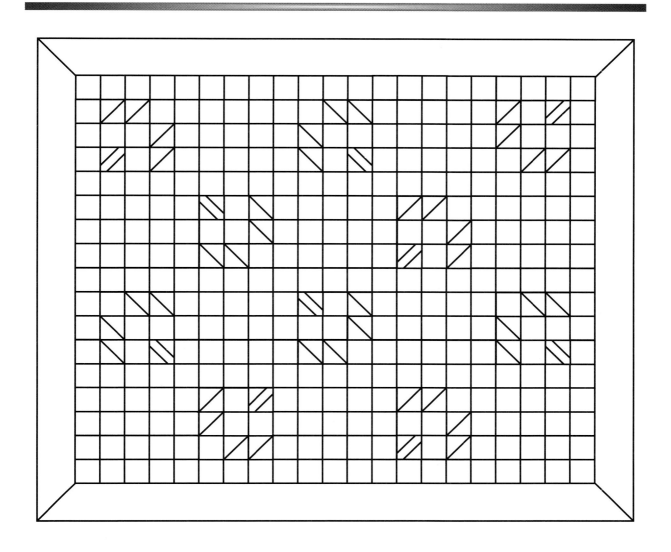

THE UGLIES

INDEX

ABOUT THE AUTHORS

JOYCE MORI

CYNTHIA TORRENCE MYERBERG

Joyce Mori is a professional quiltmaker who has written four books and over 45 articles on various aspects of quilting. She earned her Ph.D. in anthropology from the University of Missouri. Her Major area of study was North American Indian cultures, and she enjoys using Native American designs in her quilt projects. She was awarded a National Quilting Association grant to study the use of Native American designs by quilters.

Joyce started dyeing and painting her own fabrics in 1989, and she finds it very enjoyable and satisfying. Her most recent work uses her own fabrics in her Indian design quilts. She exhibits and sells her quilts at various galleries and has had her work juried into several art competitions. Quilting creations by D. J. markets quilting stencils based on her Native American designs. She offers lectures and workshops on using Native American designs in quilts as well as on dyeing and painting fabrics. She and her husband currently reside in Morgantown, West Virginia.

Cynthia Torrence Myerberg is an accomplished seamstress, quilter, and artist. After a career in nursing, she is now a returning student at West Virginia University studying art, and clothing and textiles.

Cynthia learned sewing from her mother and has always enjoyed making garments for her daughter and herself, especially couture tailored garments, evening wear and wearable art.

She has won awards for her student designs and illustrations in national and local competitions. Her quilts have also won awards in local shows. Cynthia has been making quilts for ten years. After making numerous traditional quilts, she explored ways to combine her design and painting skills with her love of fabric.

After taking a workshop on fabric dyeing from Jan Myers-Newbury in 1992, she began to explore some of the surface design techniques that she now uses to make the connection between art and craft.

Cynthia and her husband David reside in Morgantown, West Virginia.